Green Living

Practical Steps for a
Sustainable Future

By
Eco Sage

Green Living

Practical Steps for a
Sustainable Future

Table of Contents

Introduction

There's a quiet revolution happening, and it's one you can't afford to miss. It's the shift toward sustainability, a movement that's not just a buzzword but a lifeline for our planet. As we're enveloped by the consequences of our past actions—wildfires, deforestation, melting ice caps—the call for sustainable living resonates louder than ever. But this isn't a call meant to induce panic; it's a call to action, an invitation to be part of the solution.

Imagine waking up in a world where clean air and pristine waters are the norms, not the exceptions. Picture a future where communities are fueled by renewable energy, where waste is a term of the past, and where our actions don't just strip the Earth but replenish it. This book is your guide to making that vision a reality. More than just a manual, it's a journey toward adopting practices that will not only enhance your life but ensure a more livable planet for generations to come.

For an environmentally conscious individual like yourself, the term "sustainable living" might evoke images of solar panels, compost bins, or even minimalistic homes. Yet, it encompasses much more. It's an ethos, a way of life that prioritizes long-term well-being over short-term gains. This book is here to break down those concepts into actionable steps that anyone—regardless of where they are on their green journey—can implement.

But first, let's ground ourselves in the why. Why should you—or anyone for that matter—care about sustainability? The answer lies in the interconnectedness of life on Earth. Every decision we make ripples through ecosystems and economies, affecting people and species far removed from our immediate surroundings. When you choose to reduce waste, minimize your carbon footprint, or support ethical brands, you send a powerful message, nudging the world toward a more sustainable direction.

While the seriousness of environmental degradation can't be overstated, it's crucial to balance that with hope. Yes, hope. Because alongside the sobering statistics are stories of triumph, innovation, and resilience. And hope is a potent catalyst for change. Our aim is to equip you with the knowledge and tools, but more importantly, to inspire you to believe in the impact of your choices and actions.

Creating a Ripple Effect

Each chapter in this book is designed to serve a dual purpose: to educate and to inspire. We'll delve into the principles of sustainable living—guiding you through the three R's of waste management, offering insights into energy-efficient practices, and exploring eco-friendly transportation options. You'll learn about making sustainable food choices, conserving water, and transforming your home to be more eco-friendly. We'll also look into the broader scope of ethical consumerism and the vital role of community involvement.

The goal is to provide you with a holistic understanding of sustainability while focusing on practical advice. For instance, when we discuss reducing waste, we'll explore not just the 'how' but the 'why'. Understanding the implications of your actions can bolster your commitment to making changes. It's about creating a ripple effect— your changes might inspire others, leading to broader societal shifts.

It's important to note that sustainable living isn't about perfection; it's about making better choices more often. It's easy to feel overwhelmed by the enormity of the challenge, but every small, considerate action compounds to create significant positive outcomes.

Whether you're a seasoned environmentalist or a curious beginner, there's always a next step to take, a new habit to form, or an old one to refine.

The Power of Community

One of the most powerful tools we have in this journey is community. There's strength in numbers, and collective action amplifies individual efforts. Throughout this book, you'll find sections dedicated to getting involved in local environmental initiatives and leveraging community power to advocate for larger systemic changes. You'll also read inspirit-ional stories of individuals and communities making a difference. These stories aren't just heartwarming—they're proof that change is possible.

Even in your immediate circle, encouraging family, friends, or neighbors to adopt eco-friendly practices can plant seeds of change. Sharing knowledge and resources, organizing community clean-ups, or supporting local green initiatives are impactful ways to foster a culture of sustainability within your sphere of influence.

The Future is Now

As we look toward the future, the potential for continued environmental and societal transformation is both immense and exciting. Emerging green technologies promise to revolutionize the way we interact with our planet, while evolving policies and legislation aim to enforce more stringent environmental protections. However, these advances need our support and advocacy to flourish.

Throughout this guide, we'll not only explore these emerging trends but also consider how you can be an active participant in shaping this future. Grassroots movements, voting for eco-friendly policies, supporting environmental organizations—every action counts. By educating yourself and others, advocating for necessary changes, and continually striving to live more sustainably, you're contributing to a larger, global effort.

Ultimately, the path to a sustainable future is paved with collective action and individual commitment. The principles and practices outlined in this book aim to empower you to take actionable steps, however small, toward a more eco-friendly lifestyle. Each choice you make in favor of sustainability strengthens the possibility of a verdant, thriving world for ourselves and future generations.

So, are you ready to embark on this transformative journey? Let's dive into the rich and varied landscape of sustainability, armed with the knowledge that our efforts—while seemingly small at times—are fundamentally powerful. Together, we can foster a world that's not only sustainable but truly flourishing.

Chapter 1:
Understanding Sustainability

To truly grasp the concept of sustainability, one must first delve into its essence—it's about living in harmony with our environment and ensuring that our actions today don't rob future generations of their own quality of life. Sustainability isn't just about conserving resources like water and energy; it's about a holistic approach that respects the delicate balance of our ecosystems. Imagine a world where every action, big or small, contributes to a healthier planet: that's the goal. Understanding sustainability means recognizing the interconnectedness of our choices—from the food we eat to the products we consume—and how they impact the environment. By learning the fundamental principles of sustainable living and reflecting on how past generations managed to thrive while maintaining ecological balance, we empower ourselves to make meaningful, positive changes. Let's embark on this journey, opening our eyes to the possibilities and responsibilities that lie ahead.

The Principles of Sustainable Living

In this journey toward a more sustainable lifestyle, the principles of sustainable living serve as our guiding lights, showing us the path to not only reducing our environmental impact but also improving our quality of life. Adopting sustainable living practices doesn't mean making radical changes overnight. Instead, it's about incorporating thoughtful, incremental changes into our daily habits that collectively lead to significant positive outcomes.

The essence of sustainable living can be distilled into three primary principles: **reduce consumption, prioritize renewability, and foster community engagement**.

First, reducing consumption is about living more mindfully and deliberately. It's not just about using fewer resources; it's about questioning the necessity of the things we use and their lifecycle. Ask yourself: Do you really need that new outfit? Can you fix or upcycle something instead of throwing it away? By being conscious of our consumption patterns, we can drastically cut down on waste and resource use.

Second, prioritizing renewability means choosing materials and energy sources that can be replenished naturally over time. This includes everything from using solar panels for your energy needs to choosing products made from renewable resources, like bamboo or recycled materials. It's about shifting from a disposable culture to one that values longevity and sustainability.

Third, fostering community engagement recognizes that sustainability isn't an individual endeavor, but a collective one. By working with local communities, participating in environmental initiatives, and supporting local economies, we can build resilient systems that benefit both people and the planet. Community gardens, local repair cafes, and neighborhood recycling programs are all excellent examples of how community engagement can play a crucial role in sustainable living.

While these principles provide a broad framework, the practical application is where the real transformation happens. Start small. Begin with one aspect of your life — perhaps your home, transportation, or food choices — and gradually make changes that align with these principles. Each step you take, no matter how small, is a victory for sustainability.

Let's dive deeper into reducing consumption, which can take many forms. It starts with awareness and extends to active measures such as decluttering your space, adopting a minimalist approach, or even practicing digital detoxes. Think about your purchases: opt for quality over quantity, and support businesses that prioritize ethical and sustainable practices. In doing so, you'll not only reduce waste but also promote a kinder, more thoughtful consumer culture.

Renewability can take on myriad forms, from the energy sources we use to the products we choose. Renewable energy technologies like solar and wind power offer promising alternatives to fossil fuels. On a smaller scale, simple practices like choosing reusable over disposable items can make a significant impact. For instance, carrying a metal water bottle, using cloth bags for shopping, or even making your cleaning products at home can contribute significantly to reducing your carbon footprint.

Community engagement is a powerful principle that transforms thoughts into action. By connecting with like-minded individuals and groups, you can amplify your impact. Volunteer for local clean-up days or join a local environmental organization. These efforts not only help the environment but also build a sense of camaraderie and shared purpose. Strong communities can advocate for greener policies and practices more effectively than individuals acting alone.

We can't overlook the importance of education and sharing knowledge. The more we learn about the environmental impact of our choices, the better equipped we are to make changes. Read books, attend workshops, and engage in discussions about sustainability. Knowledge is power, and sharing that knowledge can inspire others to join the movement toward a more sustainable future.

Another critical component of sustainable living is resilience. Building resilient systems — whether in our homes, communities, or economies — prepares us for future challenges, from climate change to resource shortages. This might mean growing your own food, learning new skills, or investing in technologies that help mitigate environmental impacts. Resilience isn't just about survival; it's about thriving in a way that's harmonious with the planet.

Finally, remember that sustainable living is an ongoing journey. It's about progress, not perfection. Celebrate your successes, learn from your setbacks, and keep moving forward. Sustainability isn't a destination but a way of life, a series of choices made consciously and consistently to benefit both the planet and its inhabitants.

These principles are not isolated but interwoven, each supporting and enhancing the other. By reducing consumption, we make space for renewability. By prioritizing renewability, we foster a culture that values sustainability. By engaging our communities, we create a collective force for positive change. Implementing these principles in your life may start as a commitment to small daily practices, but, as they accumulate, they transform into a lifeway that's in tune with the natural world.

Your actions today will lay the groundwork for a more sustainable tomorrow. Embrace the journey with intention and heart, knowing that every positive step contributes to a larger, more meaningful impact. Sustainability isn't just a practice; it's a legacy we leave for the generations to come.

Historical Perspectives on Sustainability

Understanding the historical context of sustainability provides a richer, more nuanced appreciation of modern environmental challenges and solutions. The idea of living sustainably isn't a newfangled concept clear-cut from contemporary intellectual discourse. Far from it, communities throughout history have embraced, adapted, and sometimes clashed over the principles of harmonizing human existence with the natural world.

Ancient civilizations, whether intentionally or out of sheer necessity, adopted numerous sustainable practices. Take, for instance, the agricultural methods of ancient Egypt. Utilizing the annual flooding of the Nile River, these early innovators developed a form of farming that relied on natural irrigation and fertilization. This not only reduced the need for artificial inputs but created a self-sustaining cycle that supported one of the world's longest-lasting civilizations.

Similarly, the Indigenous peoples of North America have long practiced sustainable living methods that modern environmentalists might recognize. They operated on principles such as selective hunting and fishing, which prevented overexploitation of wildlife resources, and employed controlled burns to manage forest health and reduce wildfire risks. These practices were ingrained within their cultural and spiritual beliefs, stressing a profound connection and respect for nature that predates modern sustainability concepts.

As societies grew and technologies advanced, the balance between human activities and nature started to wobble. The Industrial Revolution, a period of rapid industrial growth from the late 18th to early 19th centuries, dramatically altered this equilibrium. While it spurred economic growth and technological advancements, it also marked the beginning of large-scale environmental degradation. Coal burning polluted the air, rivers turned toxic with industrial waste, and rapid urbanization devoured fields and forests. The Industrial Revolution is a pivotal historical moment when humanity's impact on the Earth became palpably unsustainable.

The environmental consequences of unchecked industrial growth eventually gave rise to the modern environmental movement. This awakening began in earnest during the 1960s and 1970s, catalyzed by several notable events and figures. One critical milestone was the publication of "Silent Spring" in 1962, a groundbreaking work that brought attention to the dangers of pesticides and ignited widespread public concern about environmental issues. It was one of the first instances where scientific research effectively communicated the profound impacts of human activity on natural ecosystems.

This era also saw the establishment of Earth Day in 1970, a landmark event that brought millions of Americans together to advocate for cleaner air, water, and land. It marked a collective acknowledgment that the trajectory of environmental harm needed to be addressed and halted. The momentum from this period spurred legislative actions such as the Clean Air Act, Clean Water Act, and the formation of the Environmental Protection Agency (EPA).

However, these historical efforts often wavered in the face of economic pressures and political shifts. The 1980s and 1990s witnessed a series of steps forward and back, as environmental awareness clashed with industrial and economic ambitions. Events like the Exxon Valdez oil spill in 1989 and emerging concerns about climate change reiterated the urgent need for more comprehensive and cohesive approaches to sustainability.

In recent decades, the sustainability field has evolved into a deeply interdisciplinary practice, pulling from fields as diverse as ecology, economics, and even ethics. Terms like 'sustainable development' and 'green economy' have become integral to global policy dialogues. The concept of sustainability now encompasses a broader understanding that includes social, economic, and environmental sustainability, recognizing that true sustainability cannot be achieved without balancing all three dimensions.

Historical perspectives on sustainability teach us that while technology and societies have evolved, the fundamental principles of living in harmony with nature remain consistent. Ancient methods, born out of necessity, and modern strategies, driven by advanced sciences, share common threads: the efficient use of resources, maintaining biodiversity, and understanding our obligations to future generations.

As we look back, it's enlightening to see how Indigenous knowledge and historic practices are increasingly being revisited and validated by modern science. Traditional ecological knowledge is now often integrated into modern environmental practices. For instance, permaculture, a system of agricultural and social design principles that seeks to mimic the patterns observed in natural ecosystems, draws heavily from Indigenous principles.

Another critical point drawn from history is the importance of local action and community involvement. Many historical examples of sustainable living were inherently local efforts, tailored to specific environments and communities. Modern sustainability movements have rejuvenated this localized approach, recognizing that what works for one community or ecosystem may not be suitable for another.

Understanding the history of sustainability also involves recognizing the influential role of thought leaders and activists. Throughout the decades, individuals have seized the mantle of advocating for change, from scientists and writers to politicians and grassroots activists. Their efforts have contributed to a growing global consciousness about the finite nature of our planet's resources and the interdependence of human and ecological health.

Ultimately, this historical perspective reaffirms that sustainability isn't merely an environmental or economic concern—it's a deeply human one. The continuous thread running through the fabric of human history is the recognition that our fates are tied to the health of the environment. Our challenge today is to go beyond just recognizing this truth and to build on the legacy of those who have already paved the way, using the innovative, interdisciplinary approaches at our disposal.

Harnessing the wisdom of the past, blending it with contemporary science and technology, and grounding initiatives in community and ethical practices can empower us to forge a sustainable future. The lessons drawn from the past are not just cautionary tales but also beacons of hope, highlighting the resilience of communities and the adaptability of human ingenuity.

In conclusion, historical perspectives on sustainability provide both a mirror and a map. They reflect how far we've come and guide us toward a path where humanity's progress goes hand in hand with the stewardship of our planet. As we move forward, integrating these lessons into our daily lives can help create a world where living sustainably is not an exception but the norm.

Chapter 2:
Reducing Waste

Reducing waste is more than just a practice; it's a profound commitment to reshaping our relationship with the world. When we choose to cut down on waste, we're pledging to live more thoughtfully, making deliberate choices that prioritize the planet over convenience. Imagine the impact if each of us consciously decided to buy less, reuse what we have, and recycle responsibly. By adopting these principles, we take significant strides towards mitigating the environmental damage caused by excessive consumption. In our homes, in our daily routines, the conscious effort to minimize waste cultivates a more sustainable and fulfilling way of life. This chapter will guide you through practical steps for eliminating waste, from embracing the "3 R's" to mastering tips for a zero-waste lifestyle, setting a foundation upon which even the smallest actions build a massive, positive impact.

The 3 R's: Reduce, Reuse, Recycle

Reducing waste is an essential practice in the quest for sustainability, and the approach is best encapsulated by the concept of the 3 R's: Reduce, Reuse, Recycle. Each of these components plays a crucial role in minimizing our environmental impact and fostering a healthier planet. By integrating these principles into our daily routines, we not only contribute to environmental conservation but also promote a more mindful and deliberate way of living.

Firstly, let's dive into the concept of reduction. Reducing waste means making conscious decisions to limit the amount of waste we produce from the outset. It's about choosing quality over quantity and being intentional with our purchases. When we think about reducing, consider the life cycle of products—how they're made, how long they'll last, and what will happen to them once they're no longer useful. Embracing reduction often means buying less, opting for items that have longer lifespans, and supporting companies that prioritize sustainability.

Imagine a world where disposable products are a thing of the past. Instead of single-use items, we focus on multi-use solutions that stand the test of time. Simple changes, like using a refillable water bottle instead of buying bottled water, can have a profound impact. Likewise, choosing products with minimal packaging or buying in bulk reduces the amount of waste generated from packaging materials. The goal is to minimize the input as much as possible, creating less outflow of waste.

Next, we'll explore the principle of reuse. Reusing is about extending the lifecycle of items and finding new purposes for things that might otherwise be discarded. It's a mindset shift from seeing objects as single-use to viewing them as opportunities for creativity and innovation. For example, glass jars can be repurposed for storage, old clothes can be transformed into cleaning rags, and furniture can be refurbished instead of thrown away.

The beauty of reusing is that it often sparks creativity and resourcefulness. When you start to think about how you can give items a second, third, or even fourth life, you begin to see potential in what was once considered waste. Community swaps, thrift stores, and online marketplaces can also be treasure troves for finding pre-loved items that still have plenty of utility left. By choosing to reuse, you not only reduce the demand for new products but also cut down on the need for additional raw materials and the energy required to produce new goods.

Then, there's recycling, the final R in our trio. Recycling is the process of converting waste materials into new, usable products. It's an essential component of waste reduction, albeit not as impactful as reducing and reusing. Recycling helps conserve resources, saves energy, and reduces pollution. But, it's critical to approach recycling with the understanding that it's not a cure-all solution. Not all materials are recyclable, and many recycling processes are energy-intensive.

That said, recycling is a crucial part of waste management. To make the most of it, it's important to understand local recycling guidelines and sort waste properly. Paper, cardboard, glass, certain plastics, and metals are commonly recycled materials. However, items contaminated with food waste or non-recyclable materials mixed in can disrupt the recycling process, making entire batches unusable. Proper sorting and cleaning can make a significant difference. Know what your local recycling facility accepts and do your part to ensure materials are clean and correctly sorted.

Each of the 3 R's is interconnected and reinforces the others. Reducing waste from the beginning reduces the strain on recycling processes. Reusing existing items delays their entry into the waste stream, giving recycling systems some breathing room and conserving resources. Thus, adopting a holistic approach to the 3 R's creates a robust system of waste minimization and resource conservation.

Let's not overlook the role of education and advocacy in promoting the 3 R's. Spreading awareness about the importance of reducing, reusing, and recycling is crucial. Community workshops, online resources, and educational campaigns within schools can empower individuals to take action. Being informed about the environmental impact of waste and understanding practical steps to mitigate it are powerful tools for enacting change.

Schools have a unique opportunity to instill these values in the younger generation. Practical projects like crafting with recycled materials, school-wide recycling programs, and discussions about sustainability can lay the groundwork for lifelong eco-friendly habits. When children learn the importance of the 3 R's early on, those principles often carry forward into adulthood, fostering a culture of responsibility and mindfulness.

Businesses and organizations also play a critical role. Companies can implement waste reduction strategies within their operations, such as reducing packaging, offering products made from recycled materials, and setting up take-back programs for end-of-life products. By modeling these practices, businesses not only lessen their environmental impact but also set a standard for their consumers, encouraging them to make sustainable choices.

Moreover, policy and legislation can support and amplify the efforts of individuals and organizations. Governments can implement regulations for waste reduction, recycling mandates, and incentives for businesses and consumers to adopt sustainable practices. Public policy can create the framework within which the 3 R's can thrive, driving systemic change that supports environmental conservation.

On a global scale, sharing successful strategies and technologies for waste reduction and recycling can foster collaborative efforts. By learning from one another, communities and nations can adopt best practices and innovate further. International agreements and partnerships can lend momentum to the collective effort to reduce waste and protect our planet.

Incorporating the 3 R's into our lives means continually evaluating and adjusting our habits. It's an ongoing journey rather than a one-time change. Small, consistent actions ripple out, creating significant impact over time. As we strive to reduce our waste, reuse what we can, and recycle responsibly, we contribute to a more sustainable future, one step at a time. The choices we make today will shape the world for generations to come.

Tips for a Zero-Waste Lifestyle

Embracing a zero-waste lifestyle can seem daunting, but it's all about making small, intentional changes that add up over time. Start by evaluating your daily habits and identifying areas where waste can be minimized. For instance, opting for reusable bags, bottles, and containers can significantly cut down on single-use plastics. When it comes to shopping, buy in bulk and choose products with minimal packaging or packaging that can be recycled or composted. Another effective strategy is to carry your own utensils and straws to avoid disposable ones. Additionally, be mindful of your wardrobe; try swapping clothes with friends or buying second-hand. Set up a compost bin for food scraps and yard waste to enrich your garden soil and reduce landfill contributions. With a little creativity and commitment, you can make impactful strides towards a zero-waste lifestyle, fostering a healthier planet for future generations.

Composting at Home is one of the most transformative actions you can take in your journey toward a more sustainable lifestyle. At its core, composting is nature's way of recycling. By repurposing organic waste, you turn kitchen scraps and yard trimmings into nutrient-rich soil amendments. Not only does this divert waste from landfills, but it also nurtures your garden or potted plants. Let's dive into why and how you can start composting right at home.

The beauty of composting lies in its simplicity and flexibility. You don't need an expansive backyard or a complex setup to get started. Even city dwellers in compact apartments can find ways to compost effectively. The key is to understand the basic principles of composting: balancing greens and browns, monitoring moisture, and ensuring adequate aeration. With these elements in harmony, you're well on your way to creating "black gold."

So, what exactly are greens and browns? Greens are nitrogen-rich materials like fruit peels, vegetable scraps, coffee grounds, and fresh grass clippings. Browns, on the other hand, are carbon-rich items such as dry leaves, cardboard, paper, and straw. The ratio, often suggested as 2:1 browns to greens, is crucial for maintaining the right balance, reducing odors, and speeding up decomposition. When starting your compost pile or bin, layer these materials to create a healthy mix.

If you have a backyard, setting up a compost pile or using a compost bin is quite straightforward. Choose a dry, shady spot that's easily accessible. If you're using a bin, drill holes or ensure it has slats to allow for airflow. Begin by placing a layer of coarse materials like twigs or straw at the bottom to aid in drainage. Then, alternate between greens and browns, adding kitchen scraps and garden waste as they accumulate. Give the pile a good watering and regularly turn it with a pitchfork or shovel to introduce oxygen, which is vital for the decomposition process.

For those in apartments or smaller spaces, there's no need to feel left out. Countertop compost bins and worm composting systems, also known as vermicomposting, are fantastic alternatives. A countertop bin is compact and perfect for collecting food scraps before transferring them to an outdoor bin or community compost site. Worm bins, which can be kept under the sink or on a balcony, involve special composting worms that efficiently break down organic materials. Vermicomposting not only manages your waste but also provides nutrient-dense worm castings, a powerhouse fertilizer for your plants.

Understanding the composting timeline helps manage expectations. Composting isn't an overnight process; it can take any-where from a few months to a year for materials to fully decompose into rich compost. Factors like material size, the balance of greens and browns, moisture, and how often you turn the pile all influence the speed of decomposition. Patience is key, but the eventual reward is worth the wait.

One common question is what can and can't be composted. Stick to fruit and vegetable scraps, coffee grounds, eggshells, leaves, straw, and non-glossy paper. Avoid meat, dairy, oils, and diseased plants, as they can attract pests or introduce pathogens to your compost. Pet waste should also be kept out due to potential harmful bacteria.

Moisture is another critical aspect. Your compost should have the consistency of a wrung-out sponge; too wet, and it becomes a soggy, smelly mess; too dry, and decomposition grinds to a halt. If you find your pile is too wet, add more browns and turn it more frequently. If it's too dry, incorporate more greens and give it a spritz of water.

For those looking to take their composting further, consider advanced methods like hot composting or adding compost accelerators. Hot composting involves higher temperatures to break down materials more quickly, but it requires diligent turning and monitoring. Accelerators can be purchased or made at home using ingredients like molasses to boost microbial activity.

On this newfound journey, community resources can be invaluable. Many cities offer composting workshops, provide subsidized compost bins, or have community compost facilities where you can drop off your kitchen scraps. Connecting with local community gardens or environmental groups can also provide support and additional resources.

Composting at home not only reduces your environmental footprint but serves as a daily reminder of the cyclical nature of life. Imagine the satisfaction of watching banana peels or fallen leaves transform into rich, dark compost that fuels the growth of vibrant flowers or hearty vegetables. It's a small but powerful way to engage with the natural world and make a tangible impact. As you turn your food waste into fertile ground, you're participating in a time-honored practice that benefits both you and the planet.

DIY Cleaning Products are a surprisingly simple and effective way to reduce waste while maintaining a clean and healthy home. In our quest to live more sustainably, we often overlook the everyday products that contribute to environmental degradation. Commercial cleaning products, for instance, are loaded with harmful chemicals, packaged in single-use plastics, and transported over long distances— all contributing to pollution and waste.

We have the power to change this by creating our own DIY cleaning products. These alternatives are not only environmentally friendly but also affordable and often more effective than their commercial counterparts. The beauty of making your own cleaning products lies in the control you have over the ingredients—choosing natural, non-toxic substances that are safe for your family and the planet.

One of the simplest and most versatile cleaning solutions is a mixture of vinegar and water. This combination can be used for cleaning windows, countertops, and even floors. Vinegar's acidity helps to break down grime and kills many types of bacteria. It's also a natural deodorizer. To prepare, just mix one part vinegar with one part water in a spray bottle, and you're good to go.

For those who find the smell of vinegar too strong, you can add a few drops of essential oils like lavender or eucalyptus. These not only mask the vinegar's scent but also bring their own antibacterial and antiviral properties to your cleaning regimen. Incorporating essential oils makes cleaning an aromatic experience rather than a chore.

Lemons are another powerful, natural cleaning agent. The citric acid in lemon juice is great for cutting through grease and disinfecting surfaces. Mix lemon juice with baking soda to form a paste that can scrub away tough stains on counters, stoves, and even sinks. Plus, the natural scent of lemon freshens up the space without the need for synthetic fragrances.

Speaking of baking soda, its role in DIY cleaning cannot be understated. This common household item is a powerhouse when it comes to scrubbing and deodorizing. Sprinkle it onto carpets before vacuuming to lift odors or combine it with water to create a paste that can clean everything from your bathroom tiles to your oven. The abrasive quality of baking soda makes it an excellent scrub without damaging surfaces.

Another fantastic ingredient for DIY cleaning products is castile soap. This vegetable-based soap is gentle yet effective. You can use it to make a range of cleaning solutions. For a multi-purpose cleaner, mix castile soap with water in a spray bottle. Add a few drops of tea tree oil for its antimicrobial benefits, and you've got a potent, eco-friendly cleaner on your hands.

It's crucial to remember the importance of proper storage when making DIY cleaning products. Always store your homemade solutions in reusable glass or stainless steel containers. This practice not only avoids plastic waste but also ensures that the chemicals from plastic don't leach into your natural cleaners.

Creating your cleaning products isn't just about sustainability; it's also about reconnecting with simpler, safer ways of doing things. You'll find that you need fewer products than you think to keep your home sparkly clean. Let's delve into a few more specific recipes that you can easily whip up in your kitchen:

All-Purpose Cleaner: Combine 1 cup of water, 1 cup of distilled white vinegar, and 10-15 drops of essential oil of your choice in a spray bottle. Shake well before use. This cleaner works on most surfaces but avoid using it on granite or marble, as vinegar can etch natural stone.

Glass Cleaner: Mix 1 part water with 1 part vinegar and a splash of rubbing alcohol in a spray bottle. This solution leaves windows and mirrors streak-free and sparkling.

Bathroom Cleaner: Combine 1 cup of baking soda, 1/4 cup of castile soap, and a few drops of tea tree oil. Apply the paste to your sink, tub, and tiles, then scrub away grime and mildew.

Furniture Polish: Mix 1/4 cup of olive oil with 1/4 cup of vinegar and a few drops of lemon essential oil. Apply with a soft cloth to wood furniture to bring out its natural shine.

The financial benefits of DIY cleaning products are equally significant. Many of the ingredients like baking soda, vinegar, and essential oils are cost-effective and multipurpose. By making your products, you can save a considerable amount of money over time, which is an added bonus to their sustainability benefits.

Beyond the immediate financial and environmental benefits, there's something deeply satisfying about self-sufficiency. Knowing that you have taken control over what is in your home and made decisions that benefit the planet is empowering. It also allows you to share knowledge and inspire others to make similar changes. Imagine friends and family visiting your home and experiencing the fresh, clean environment you've created using nothing more than what's in your pantry.

Transitioning to DIY cleaning products may require a slight adjustment period as you experiment with different recipes and find what works best for your needs. But, the transition is worth it. You'll quickly realize that the simplified approach doesn't compromise effectiveness. Instead, it enhances your connection to the actions you take daily in maintaining your home.

DIY doesn't have to mean completely from scratch every time, either. There are various pre-mixed natural products available that can bolster your sustainable cleaning efforts while saving time. Consider integrating these into your regimen for more convenience without straying from your eco-friendly ethos.

In conclusion, taking the time to create your own cleaning products merges practical sustainability with everyday living. It reduces waste, avoids harmful chemicals, and empowers you as a steward of the Earth. It's a tangible action within your grasp that contributes to larger environmental conservation efforts. This journey toward greener cleaning is one step among many, but every step counts in our collective stride towards a more sustainable future.

As we move forward, keep exploring other facets of sustainable living, and remember, the smallest changes can have a significant impact when they become part of our daily lives. Next, we will delve into composting at home, another incredibly effective way to reduce waste and live harmoniously with our environment.

Chapter 3:
Minimizing Carbon Footprint

Weaving sustainability into our daily lives requires careful stewardship of the earth's resources, especially when it comes to slashing our carbon emissions. Reducing your carbon footprint isn't just a lofty goal—it's a tangible challenge that starts with small, decisive steps. From opting for energy-efficient lighting and appliances to carpooling or biking instead of driving solo, every action matters. Imagine your home as a sanctuary of efficiency, harnessing the power of the sun through solar panels or smartly insulating walls to keep your heating and cooling systems from working overtime. This chapter offers practical advice on how you can make a substantial difference. Remember, the goal is to create a ripple effect—small changes in your everyday routines can contribute to larger, community-wide impacts, encouraging others to follow suit. Let's embark on this journey together to minimize our carbon outputs and usher in a cleaner, greener future for generations to come.

Calculating Your Carbon Footprint

To truly minimize your carbon footprint, it's crucial to first understand what that footprint looks like. Calculating your carbon footprint might sound daunting, but it's an essential step in gauging the impact of your daily activities and making more eco-conscious choices. Knowing is half the battle, and once you grasp where your emissions are coming from, you can make targeted changes that have a real impact.

So, what exactly is a carbon footprint? In essence, it's the total amount of greenhouse gases—including carbon dioxide, methane, nitrous oxide, and fluorinated gases—that you're responsible for emitting into the atmosphere. These emissions come from a variety of sources, ranging from the electricity you use to power your home to the gas that fuels your car, and even the food you consume.

It's important to approach this process with a sense of curiosity rather than guilt. You're not here to beat yourself up over past choices but to empower yourself with the knowledge to make better ones moving forward. Many online calculators offer a straightforward way to estimate your carbon footprint. They typically ask for information about your home energy use, transportation habits, diet, and shopping preferences. With just a few minutes of your time, you can get a pretty accurate snapshot of your carbon emissions.

One of the simplest ways to start is by focusing on your energy consumption. Take a look at your monthly electricity and gas bills. They often provide a breakdown of your energy use which can be converted into carbon emissions. Multiple online resources can help with these calculations. For instance, using an online carbon calculator, you might input your average monthly electricity usage in kilowatt-hours (kWh) and receive an estimate of how many tons of CO_2 you're responsible for each year just from powering your home.

Transportation is another major contributor to your carbon footprint. If you drive a car, the type of vehicle, the fuel it uses, and how often you drive will all factor in. Calculate the number of miles you typically commute and any additional driving you do for errands or leisure. If you take flights, these can be significant as well; even one or two long-haul flights per year can substantially increase your overall emissions. Again, online calculators can make this easy by offering options to enter the distance of your flights and the type of travel (economy class, business class, etc.) to give a more tailored estimate.

Have you ever considered the impact of the food you eat? What you put on your plate can have a surprisingly large impact on your carbon footprint. Meat, especially beef and lamb, generally has a higher carbon footprint compared to plant-based foods. This is due to the methane emissions from livestock, as well as the resources required to grow their feed. A detailed evaluation of your diet, looking at how often you eat meat, dairy, and processed foods compared to vegetables, fruits, and grains, can reveal important insights. Reducing meat consumption even slightly or choosing sustainably sourced foods can make a significant difference.

Then there's your shopping habits. Every product you purchase, from clothes to electronics, comes with its own carbon cost—from the raw materials and manufacturing process to shipping and packaging. Fast fashion, for instance, churns through significant resources and produces a lot of waste. By tracking your purchases and noting the origin of products, you can begin to understand the hidden emissions tied to your consumer behavior. You might not be able to stop buying everything, but you can switch to more sustainable brands and mindful shopping practices to lessen your footprint.

Now, armed with this information, it's time to take stock of the results. You'll likely find that some areas are more significant than others. Identifying these high-impact areas helps you prioritize where to focus your efforts. For instance, if your transportation emissions are sky-high due to daily driving, perhaps exploring carpooling, public transportation, or even an electric vehicle can have the biggest immediate effect. Conversely, if home energy use is your main contributor, tackling energy efficiency might be the best first step.

Starting small can make the process more manageable. You don't need to overhaul your entire life overnight. Each small change, whether it's switching to energy-efficient bulbs, cutting down on meat one meal a week, or biking instead of driving occasionally, adds up. It's the accumulation of these seemingly minor shifts that leads to substantial reductions in your carbon footprint over time.

Feel encouraged that every step you take toward lowering your carbon footprint is a step toward a healthier planet. As you measure and adjust, you'll not only see your numbers go down, but you'll also become more attuned to the environmental impacts of daily choices. And don't forget to revisit your calculations periodically. Life changes, and so do our habits. Regularly updating your carbon footprint assessment ensures you remain on track and continually moving in the right direction.

In time, these practices become second nature. The goal is not just to minimize your carbon footprint but to ingrain sustainability into your daily life—creating a ripple effect that encourages others to do the same. By making more informed choices, you're contributing to a larger movement of people dedicated to preserving our planet for future generations.

In the next section, we'll delve deeper into tangible steps for making your home more energy-efficient, which can drastically cut down on your carbon emissions. But for now, take a moment to reflect on what you've learned about your carbon footprint. Use this newfound insight as a foundation on your journey toward a more sustainable and fulfilling lifestyle.

Energy-Efficient Homes

Transforming your home into an energy-efficient sanctuary is not just a trend; it's a crucial step in minimizing your carbon footprint. By focusing on energy efficiency, you're not only saving money on utility bills but also significantly reducing greenhouse gas emissions. Simple actions like upgrading to LED light bulbs, sealing leaks, and using programmable thermostats can make a big difference. Additionally, investing in energy-efficient appliances and considering smart home technologies can further enhance your efforts. Imagine the ripple effect: more efficient homes lead to less demand for energy production, which in turn, reduces the burning of fossil fuels. In essence, every step you take toward an energy-efficient home is a step toward a healthier planet. Start small, stay committed, and watch the positive impact on both your wallet and the environment. Your home can be a beacon of sustainability, lighting the way for others to follow suit.

Renewable Energy Sources are a potent force in reducing our carbon footprints and taking meaningful steps toward a more sustainable lifestyle. By harnessing energy that naturally replenishes itself, such as sunlight, wind, and geothermal heat, we redirect our dependence away from non-renewable and polluting fossil fuels. This transition not only benefits the planet but also provides long-term financial savings and energy security for households.

Let's start with solar energy, one of the more accessible and widely implemented renewable sources. Installing solar panels on your rooftop can transform your home into a mini power plant capturing sunlight and converting it into electricity. Over time, this initial investment pays off, reducing electric bills and lowering dependency on grid power. But that's not all. Net metering allows homeowners to sell excess electricity back to the grid, offering not just environmental benefits but also financial rewards.

What about wind energy? Though generally associated with large-scale wind farms, small wind turbines designed for residential use are becoming more commonplace. If you live in an area blessed with consistent wind flow, installing a small turbine could provide supplementary power to your home. The key is to conduct thorough research on local wind patterns and check zoning regulations before investing in wind technology.

Geothermal energy is another promising source. While its implementation can be more complex and costly upfront, it's a brilliant option for those building new homes or undergoing major renovations. Geothermal systems harness the earth's constant underground temperature to heat and cool your living spaces. This method is highly efficient, reducing energy consumption significantly and offering a quiet, low-maintenance alternative to traditional HVAC systems.

The allure of hydropower can't be ignored, either. Small-scale hydropower systems, often referred to as micro-hydro, can generate electricity for individual properties if they have access to flowing water. This option is less feasible for urban environments but can be a game-changer for rural and off-grid communities.

When considering these renewable energy sources, it's essential to factor in location, budget, and long-term needs. Solar might be ideal for sunnier climates, while geothermal could be better suited for regions with more extreme seasonal temperature variations. Wind and hydro will depend largely on geographical and natural features of the landscape. Tailoring the approach allows you to capture the maximum benefits of each resource, effectively addressing your specific circumstances.

The clear environmental benefits of adopting renewable energy are compelling, but so are the personal impacts. Think about the reduced energy bills, decreased carbon footprint, and even the potential to earn money by generating excess power. You take an active role in the energy ecosystem, promoting a cleaner, greener planet and fostering energy independence. Sometimes, it's the small changes, combined with community efforts, that drive significant impact.

Collectively, renewable energy sources transform communities. When neighborhoods, cities, or even whole regions commit to sustainable energy practices, the ripple effects are profound. Public infrastructure powered by solar panels, wind farms dotting the landscape, and community geothermal projects can contribute to a greener, more resilient energy network.

Change, especially at a community level, often begins with individual initiative. Engaging with local government and policy makers to support renewable energy projects can amplify your personal efforts. Advocate for solar incentives, community wind projects, or geothermal feasibility studies. Collaboration often leads to more substantial achievements than solo efforts, creating a cumulative force for environmental stewardship.

Moreover, educational outreach is key. Sharing your experiences and successes with renewable energy can inspire others to follow suit. Social media, local workshops, and community groups provide platforms to disseminate information and encourage widespread adoption of sustainable energy solutions. Visibility and transparency can demystify the process, making it more accessible for those on the fence.

Remember, the path to renewable energy is not an isolated journey. It's about creating a connected, empowered, and environmentally conscious community. Whether you're installing solar panels or advocating for renewable energy policies, every effort counts. Utilizing the natural resources at our disposal responsibly ensures a sustainable future (and a healthier planet) for generations to come.

Insulation and Weatherproofing can dramatically transform the energy efficiency of your home, cutting down on heating and cooling costs while reducing your carbon footprint. In the journey towards a more sustainable future, effective insulation and weatherproofing provide simple, actionable techniques that lead to significant energy savings. But it's not just about economics; it's about creating a comfortable, eco-friendly living space that harmonizes with the environment.

Imagine a home that maintains a constant, comfortable temperature with minimal energy input. Effective insulation is key to achieving this. Insulation works by reducing the transfer of heat between the inside and outside of your home, which reduces the need for artificial heating and cooling. Think of it as wrapping your home in a cozy blanket that keeps the warmth in during the cold months and the heat out during the hot months. There's a wide range of eco-friendly insulation materials available, including recycled denim, sheep's wool, and cellulose made from recycled paper.

Choosing the right insulation material can make a world of difference. Recycled denim, for example, is not only highly effective but also repurposes materials that would otherwise end up in a landfill. Similarly, sheep's wool is a natural, renewable resource that offers excellent thermal and acoustic properties. Cellulose insulation, derived from recycled newspaper, is another fantastic option. These materials provide excellent insulation while reducing waste and supporting sustainable practices.

Equally important to insulation is weatherproofing. Weatherproofing complements insulation by sealing gaps, cracks, and other openings where air can leak in or out of your home. Even the best insulation can't perform effectively if your home is rife with drafts. Common areas where leaks occur include doors, windows, and around electrical outlets. By addressing these vulnerabilities, you can significantly enhance your home's energy efficiency and comfort levels.

One of the simplest and most effective weatherproofing techniques is caulking. Caulking involves sealing gaps and cracks in your home's exterior and interior with a flexible material that can withstand varying temperatures. It's a low-cost, high-impact solution that can be easily accomplished in a weekend. Another straightforward method is weatherstripping, which involves sealing the moving parts of doors and windows to prevent drafts. Both of these techniques can help retain heat during the winter and keep your home cool during the summer.

If you live in an older home, consider doing a thorough energy audit to identify areas where insulation and weatherproofing improvements are most needed. This audit can often be done by professionals, but there are also DIY kits available for those who prefer a hands-on approach. Sometimes, even the addition of simple, removable items like draft stoppers for doors can make a noticeable difference.

Don't overlook the role of your roof and attic in insulation and weatherproofing. Heat rises, and a poorly insulated roof or attic can be a significant source of energy loss. Consider adding or upgrading the insulation in your attic and ensure that your roof is in good condition, free of leaks and properly ventilated. If you're considering a complete roof replacement, look into eco-friendly options like green roofs or roofs made from recycled materials.

Windows are another critical component in the insulation and weatherproofing equation. Double or triple-glazed windows offer superior insulation compared to single-pane windows, significantly reducing heat transfer. If new windows are not in your immediate plans, consider adding storm windows or using insulating window films as a more economical alternative. Heavy curtains or thermal blinds can also provide an extra layer of insulation.

Beyond the building itself, planting trees and shrubs around your home can serve as a natural form of weatherproofing. Strategically placed greenery can act as windbreaks in the winter and provide shade during the summer, further reducing your reliance on artificial heating and cooling. This approach not only improves your home's energy efficiency but also promotes biodiversity and beautifies your environment.

While it might seem overwhelming to tackle insulation and weatherproofing, remember that it's a gradual process. You don't have to do everything at once. Each small step you take, be it sealing a window or adding attic insulation, contributes to a more energy-efficient and sustainable home. Moreover, these efforts can yield immediate rewards in the form of lower energy bills and a more comfortable living space.

It's essential to consider insulation and weatherproofing not just as home improvement projects but as integral parts of a broader commitment to sustainability. Every action to weatherproof and insulate is a statement of intent to live in harmony with the planet. By minimizing energy waste, you're reducing your home's carbon emissions, conserving valuable resources, and taking meaningful steps towards a greener future.

Lifestyle changes accompany these physical improvements. For instance, regular maintenance, such as reapplying caulk or checking the seals on doors and windows, should become a routine part of household upkeep. Mindfulness in daily energy usage, like adjusting the thermostat by a few degrees or using energy-efficient lighting, further complements your insulation and weatherproofing efforts.

Ultimately, insulation and weatherproofing bring us back to a core principle of sustainability: working with and not against the environment. Rather than relying on exorbitant amounts of energy to create a comfortable home, we can make wise choices in materials and methods to naturally regulate our living spaces. It's a proactive, empowering path that aligns with the essence of sustainable living.

So, as you embark or continue on your journey towards sustainability, consider how you can optimize your home's insulation and weatherproofing. Whether it's choosing eco-friendly materials, sealing drafts, or adding insulation to overlooked areas, each step you take is a stride towards energy independence and environmental stewardship. The cumulative effect, shared among many households, can lead to significant positive change. Embrace these changes, and you'll find not only a more comfortable home but also a deeper connection with the world around you.

Chapter 4:
Eco-Friendly Transportation

Transitioning to eco-friendly transportation isn't just a savvy move; it's a vital step toward reducing our carbon footprints and fostering a healthier planet. Imagine replacing solo car rides with public transit, carpooling, or even opting for electric and hybrid vehicles. These choices collectively cut down emissions dramatically. Don't forget the simplicity and power of cycling and walking; they not only diminish environmental impact but also promote personal well-being. Start integrating these practices into your daily routines, and you'll find yourself contributing significantly to a cleaner, greener world. Making these shifts in how we move through life builds momentum for larger-scale change, encouraging communities and cities to develop even more sustainable infrastructure. Join this movement, and be part of the solution that future generations will thank us for.

Benefits of Public Transit

When it comes to reducing our carbon footprint and embracing an eco-friendly lifestyle, public transit plays a critical role. Many environmentally conscious individuals might already be familiar with the obvious benefits—like reducing the number of cars on the road—but the real advantages extend much further. Public transportation systems have the potential to reshape communities, mitigate environmental degradation, and offer accessible options for all economic groups.

First and foremost, public transit dramatically cuts down greenhouse gas emissions. Cars are a major source of carbon emissions, and every mile traveled by a vehicle translates into more pollutants released into the atmosphere. In contrast, buses, subways, and trams are designed to carry multiple passengers, distributing the environmental cost among many riders rather than just one driver. If you take the bus instead of driving, your personal carbon footprint could be reduced by a significant margin.

Moreover, public transit systems use less energy per passenger mile than private vehicles. By utilizing shared resources efficiently, they can operate more sustainably. Modern innovations have made buses and trains even more eco-friendly with the introduction of electric and hybrid models that further minimize their environmental impact. It's not just about cutting emissions; it's about using resources judiciously.

The infrastructure supporting public transit is also beneficial to the environment. Well-planned transit systems reduce the need for extensive road networks and sprawling parking lots, which can be detrimental to natural habitats. By limiting urban sprawl and conserving land, public transportation helps preserve green spaces and biodiversity. When fewer roads and parking lots are needed, there's more room for parks, community gardens, and other green areas.

Economic benefits shouldn't be overlooked either. Public transit can save individuals money. Owning and maintaining a vehicle is expensive—think insurance, fuel, repairs, and the initial purchase price. Public transportation offers a cost-effective alternative, particularly for those who live in urban areas. Lower transportation costs can free up funds for other sustainable investments, such as organic food or renewable energy solutions.

It's also worth considering the social benefits of public transit. It offers mobility solutions for people who can't drive, whether due to financial constraints, disabilities, or age. This inclusivity ensures that everyone has access to transportation, fostering a more equitable community. Public transit can bring neighborhoods together, making it easier for people to participate in local events, visit parks, and engage with their community. It's a system that serves to connect rather than isolate.

The health benefits associated with public transportation should not be underestimated. Reduced car usage leads to less air pollution, which in turn lowers the prevalence of respiratory issues such as asthma. Cleaner air improves overall public health, reducing healthcare costs and enhancing quality of life. Additionally, walking to and from transit stops adds a bit of physical activity to daily routines, encouraging a more active lifestyle. Over time, these small steps can contribute significantly to personal well-being.

Public transit systems themselves can be a source of education and awareness. Advertisements and campaigns on buses and trains can inform passengers about other eco-friendly practices, creating a ripple effect that extends well beyond the commute. Imagine reading about composting or renewable energy while on your daily ride—it's a subtle yet effective way to keep sustainability in the forefront of people's minds.

Let's not forget the convenience factor. High-quality public transit can actually be more convenient than driving. No more hunting for parking or getting stuck in traffic. Transit networks that are well-integrated and timely can make commuting stress-free and even enjoyable. When you're not behind the wheel, you can use that time to relax, read, or even catch up on work, making productive use of every minute.

In terms of long-term sustainability, public transit systems are adaptable. As cities grow and change, transportation networks can be adjusted more easily than roadways. New lines can be added, routes can be optimized, and services can be enhanced to meet the demands of a growing population. This flexibility ensures that public transit remains a viable and effective solution for future generations.

There's also something inherently empowering about using public transit. It's a tangible step you can take to reduce your environmental impact. Every time you choose the bus or the train over your car, you're making a statement that aligns with your values. It's a daily act of environmental conservation, a small but significant way to contribute to the health of our planet.

In conclusion, the benefits of public transit extend far beyond reducing car emissions. It fosters cleaner air, conserves valuable land, saves money, promotes inclusivity, and enhances community well-being. By integrating more public transportation into our daily lives, we contribute to a more sustainable future. Let's embrace public transit as a cornerstone of eco-friendly transportation and inspire others to do the same. Together, we can make a significant impact, one ride at a time.

Electric and Hybrid Vehicles

Electric and hybrid vehicles represent a significant leap forward in the journey toward sustainable transportation. These innovative modes of travel are not just mechanical marvels; they are catalysts for a cleaner, greener future. Let's delve into what makes them essential in the shift away from fossil fuels and how they can seamlessly integrate into your daily life, lowering your carbon footprint and enhancing environmental well-being.

First and foremost, the stark reduction in greenhouse gas emissions sets electric and hybrid vehicles apart from traditional internal combustion engine vehicles. Electric vehicles (EVs) produce zero tailpipe emissions, and hybrids greatly reduce the amount of emissions by combining a gasoline or diesel engine with an electric motor. This ensures fewer pollutants like carbon dioxide, nitrogen oxides, and particulate matter get released into the atmosphere. These emissions are major contributors to air pollution and climate change. By adopting an electric or hybrid vehicle, you can directly contribute to cleaner air and a healthier planet.

One of the misconceptions about electric vehicles is that they lack performance. On the contrary, many EV models offer torque and acceleration that rival and sometimes surpass those of their gasoline-powered counterparts. Imagine gliding silently through city streets and having instant acceleration at your command. This isn't a distant possibility—it's the reality of modern electric vehicle technology.

The widespread adoption of electric and hybrid vehicles brings us closer to energy independence. Relying more on renewable energy sources like solar or wind to charge EVs can break our dependence on imported oil, fostering a more stable and resilient energy market. It's fascinating to consider that you could drive a car powered entirely by the rays of the sun. This synergy between renewable energy and electric transportation is not just futuristic but also incredibly practical.

If you're worried about the range of electric vehicles, it's worth noting that significant advancements have been made in battery technology. Modern electric vehicles can travel 200-300 miles or more on a single charge, which is more than adequate for daily commutes and most road trips. Charging infrastructure is expanding rapidly too, with more public charging stations being installed in urban areas, along highways, and even in residential neighborhoods. It's increasingly easy to find a place to recharge, making range anxiety a thing of the past.

Hybrid vehicles offer an excellent transition for those not quite ready to go fully electric. With a hybrid, you get the best of both worlds: the convenience of gasoline for longer drives and the efficiency of electric power for shorter, everyday trips. Hybrids typically have regenerative braking systems, which capture energy typically lost during braking and use it to recharge the battery. This efficient energy use means fewer trips to the gas station, saving you money and reducing your environmental impact.

In terms of cost, it's true that electric and hybrid vehicles often come with a higher upfront price tag. But let's break this down realistically. Over the life of the vehicle, you'll save significantly on fuel and maintenance costs. Electric vehicles have fewer moving parts, meaning less wear and tear and fewer repairs. Government incentives and rebates can also help offset the initial purchase cost, making these vehicles more accessible for everyone.

Think about the implications for future generations. By adopting electric and hybrid vehicles today, you're contributing to ongoing demand and development in this sector. As technology continues to improve and economies of scale are realized, prices are expected to drop, making eco-friendly transportation an option for an even broader audience. Every electric or hybrid vehicle on the road is a step toward a more sustainable future, not just for ourselves but for our children and grandchildren.

It's also worth mentioning the enhancing role of smart technology in electric and hybrid vehicles. Features like regenerative braking, eco-driving modes, and intelligent routing not only make driving more enjoyable but also maximize energy efficiency. Vehicles equipped with these features smartly manage power distribution, ensuring that energy isn't wasted, and emissions are minimized. This is particularly impactful in urban settings where stop-and-go traffic can otherwise lead to inefficiency.

Businesses are also playing their part. Ride-sharing companies and delivery services are transitioning to electric and hybrid fleets in an effort to reduce their carbon footprints. This shift not only has significant environmental benefits but also sets a precedent that can influence consumer behavior and policy development. When people see electric vehicles in everyday use, it normalizes this eco-friendly practice, making it more likely to be adopted on a wider scale.

Incorporating electric and hybrid vehicles into your lifestyle might seem like a small change, but it collectively leads to substantial environmental benefits. Each choice we make in favor of sustainability compounds with others, creating a ripple effect that can lead to widespread change.

The time has come to embrace these advancements. Thoughtful decisions about the vehicles we drive can significantly reduce our environmental impact. When you next consider an automotive purchase, let the environment guide your choice. We've got the technology; now it's up to us to adopt it for the betterment of our planet.

Cycling and Walking

In today's fast-paced world, finding ways to live more sustainably can seem challenging. However, sometimes the most impactful changes are the simplest ones. Cycling and walking are two of the most eco-friendly modes of transportation available, combining health benefits with a significant reduction in carbon emissions. By choosing to cycle or walk instead of driving, you're making a powerful statement for environmental conservation.

Cycling, for instance, is more than just a means of getting from point A to point B. It's a comprehensive lifestyle choice that promotes well-being while reducing your ecological footprint. Modern cities around the world have recognized the importance of cycling and have started to build infrastructure that supports cyclists. Bike lanes, bike-sharing programs, and safe storage facilities have become more common, making it easier for people to make the switch.

Urban planners often emphasize the multifaceted benefits of cycling. Traffic congestion is reduced, air quality improves, and public spaces become more vibrant. The simplicity of cycling—just you, your bike, and the road—adds to its appeal. Moreover, maintenance for a bicycle is minimal compared to a car, saving you both time and money.

Walking is another fantastic eco-friendly transportation option. Often overlooked in discussions about sustainable living, walking is the most accessible form of transportation. You don't need any special equipment, and it's completely free. Walking offers unique opportunities to connect with your surroundings, providing a different experience of your community that can be both grounding and invigorating.

For those who are able, integrating walking into your daily routines can make a significant difference. Whether it's a short stroll to the grocery store or a longer walk to work, every step you take helps reduce greenhouse gas emissions. Walking lets you appreciate the local flora and fauna, discover new aspects of your neighborhood, and engage in regular physical activity, which is crucial for long-term health.

Transitioning to a lifestyle that prioritizes cycling and walking can start with small, manageable changes. Begin by identifying errands or daily activities you can accomplish without a car. Perhaps you can cycle to work a few days a week or walk to nearby shops instead of driving. Gradually, these habits become second nature, turning your daily commute into an opportunity for exercise and environmental stewardship.

Moreover, the benefits of walking and cycling extend beyond just the individual. Communities that foster walking and biking tend to be more cohesive, as these activities often encourage people to interact with one another. Local businesses also thrive in walkable areas because people are more likely to stop and explore shops and restaurants when they're on foot or a bike.

Cycling and walking can also be integrated into various aspects of community planning. Urban design that prioritizes pedestrians and cyclists can make a city not only more eco-friendly but also more vibrant and enjoyable. Spaces designed for people rather than cars usually include more green areas, parks, and public gatherings, improving the overall quality of life for residents.

The environmental impact of cycling and walking cannot be overstated. Every mile not driven by a car means fewer emissions released into the atmosphere. For environmentally conscious individuals, the choice to walk or cycle wherever possible aligns closely with the broader goal of living sustainably. By setting an example, you also inspire others to consider these modes of transportation, creating a ripple effect that benefits the community and the planet.

Incorporating these habits into your daily routine might require a shift in mindset. The convenience of driving can be hard to give up, but the long-term benefits make it worthwhile. Think of it as investing in your health and the future of the planet. As you start to see the positive impacts, staying motivated becomes easier.

To facilitate this transition, consider joining local cycling clubs or walking groups. These communities offer support, introduce you to new routes, and make the activity more social and enjoyable. Being part of a group also provides safety in numbers, which can be reassuring if you're new to urban cycling or walking long distances.

Safety is an important aspect to consider when choosing to cycle or walk. Always wear a helmet while cycling, follow traffic rules, and make yourself visible to motorists. Reflective clothing and proper lights can make a big difference during early morning or evening rides.

Similarly, walking along well-lit paths and being mindful of your surroundings ensure a safer experience.

Innovative solutions and technology can also enhance your cycling and walking experience. Apps that track your route and progress, indicate the most bike-friendly paths, or even offer bike-sharing options can make a huge difference in convenience and safety. Staying informed about new infrastructure developments in your area can open up new opportunities for vehicular alternatives.

There are also broader social and political implications. Advocating for better pedestrian and cycling infrastructure in your community can lead to systemic change. Attend town hall meetings, participate in community planning sessions, and voice your support for bike lanes, pedestrian paths, and traffic calming measures. Even small contributions can nudge cities toward more sustainable urban planning.

One step at a time, one pedal at a time, we can move towards a greener, healthier, and more connected world. Let's embrace cycling and walking not just as transportation choices but as bold lifestyle commitments that strengthen our bond with the environment and each other.

Ultimately, every journey begins in the mind. It's about making a conscious decision to choose more sustainable options, even when they require a bit more effort. By integrating walking and cycling into our lives, we're not just moving across the landscape—we're changing it. And that's the essence of eco-friendly transportation.

Chapter 5:
Sustainable Food Choices

Embracing sustainable food choices isn't just about transforming what's on your plate; it's about cultivating a deeper connection with the earth. Prioritizing local and organic produce reduces carbon emissions from transportation and minimizes harmful pesticides that damage our ecosystems. Even small changes, like having a meat-free day each week or starting a home garden, can significantly impact our planet's health. Imagine picking fresh vegetables from your backyard or supporting farmers who care for the soil and water. By choosing sustainably, we nourish ourselves and the environment, creating a cycle of care and respect that fosters a thriving planet for future generations. It's not only about eating but about living with intention and making mindful decisions that resonate beyond the dinner table.

Buying Local and Organic

Sustainable food choices are vital not only to our health but also to the health of the planet. One of the most impactful decisions we can make is to buy local and organic. These choices enhance our connection to our food supply and contribute to a more sustainable future.

Buying local means purchasing foods produced close to home. Local foods haven't traveled thousands of miles, thereby reducing the carbon footprint associated with transporting goods over long distances. When you choose local, you're not just minimizing environmental harm; you're also investing in your community. Dollars spent at local farms and markets typically stay within the community, fostering economic resilience and sustaining jobs.

Organic foods, on the other hand, are grown without the use of synthetic pesticides, fertilizers, or genetically modified organisms (GMOs). Organic farming practices prioritize soil health, water conservation, and animal welfare. Unlike conventional agriculture, organic farming builds up the soil rather than depletes it, creating a more resilient ecosystem capable of sustaining itself over the long term.

Imagine walking through a local farmers' market on a sunny morning. The air is filled with the rich scent of fresh produce and baked goods. You might meet farmers who can tell you the story behind your food, from the seed to the table. It's a living, breathing testament to the power of localized food systems. Beyond the sensory experience, this setting offers transparency that large-scale commercial operations can't match. Knowing where your food comes from helps you make informed decisions that align with your values.

Purchasing local and organic food does not have to be prohibitively expensive. Community-Supported Agriculture (CSA) programs offer an excellent way to receive fresh, seasonal produce throughout the year at a fraction of the cost you'd pay in a traditional supermarket. By subscribing to a CSA, you commit to buying a "share" of a farm's harvest in advance. This helps farmers with up-front costs and ensures you receive a steady supply of fresh produce.

Here is a simple breakdown for recognizing the benefits of local and organic purchases:

- **Improved Nutrition:** Fresh produce harvested at peak ripeness retains more nutrients than food picked early and shipped long distances.

- **Environmental Protection:** Organic farming avoids synthetic chemicals that can runoff and pollute waterways.

- **Economic Support:** Local buying keeps your money in the community, supporting regional growth and job creation.

- **Animal Welfare:** Organic standards often require more humane treatment of farm animals.

Organic farming does carry its own set of challenges, such as lower yields and higher labor costs. However, these challenges are opportunities for innovation and adaptation. Some farmers use a blend of traditional knowledge and modern techniques to create robust farming systems that are both productive and sustainable. Moreover, practices like crop rotation, polyculture, and natural pest control methods are central to organic farming and help create a balanced ecosystem.

When you buy from local and organic sources, you can also considerably reduce food waste. Local produce tends to have a longer shelf life because it's fresher when you buy it. Supermarkets often choose varieties that endure long shipping times over taste and nutritional value. In contrast, locally grown foods offer superior flavor and a shorter time from farm to table, leading to less food spoiling in your kitchen.

Even for items that can't be grown locally, choosing organic still makes a significant difference. Consider coffee or chocolate, where opting for organic versions helps combat deforestation and promotes fair labor practices. These choices resonate beyond your immediate environment, contributing to global sustainability efforts.

Let us not overlook the cultural richness that comes from buying local. Your local farmers' market is often a melting pot of culinary traditions and ethnic diversity. Seasonal foods allow you to explore new recipes and cuisines, making your meals not just healthier but also more interesting and varied.

For those living in food deserts, where access to fresh, local, and organic food is limited, change often starts with grassroots efforts. Urban farming initiatives and local cooperatives can make a huge difference. Community gardens and educational programs can spark the interest and knowledge necessary to grow food self-sufficiently, even in smaller urban spaces.

Building a habit of buying local and organic takes time, but it is rewarding in numerous ways. It opens up avenues for personal growth as you learn more about your food, the people who grow it, and the environmental impact of your choices. This lifestyle shift also serves as a powerful example to those around you, inspiring them to consider more sustainable choices in their own lives.

Transitioning to buying local and organic doesn't have to happen overnight. Start small, perhaps by dedicating one day each week to eating local meals. Gradually increase your commitment as you become more comfortable and aware of the benefits. It's not about perfection but progress.

In summary, the benefits of buying local and organic food stretch far beyond personal health. They encompass environmental steward-ship, community engagement, and economic resilience. By making conscious choices about where and how we buy our food, we play our part in shaping a more sustainable, equitable world.

Reducing Meat Consumption

As we explore the realm of sustainable food choices, one significant step towards a greener lifestyle is reducing meat consumption. It's not just a matter of diet; it's a powerful statement of our commitment to environmental stewardship. The impact of meat production on our planet is multifaceted and profound, involving land use, water consumption, and greenhouse gas emissions. But the good news is that even small changes can lead to significant benefits.

Many of us have grown up with meat being a central part of our diet. It's culturally ingrained and often seen as a symbol of prosperity and health. But times are changing, and with them, our understanding of sustainability. Studies indicate that meat production is one of the largest contributors to environmental degradation. Livestock farming requires vast amounts of land, mostly for growing feed crops. This leads to deforestation and loss of biodiversity, which are critical issues we can't ignore.

Take beef production, for instance. It's notorious for its high environmental cost. To produce just one pound of beef, approx.-imately 1,800 gallons of water are required. That's an absolutely staggering amount when you think about it! Contrast this with plant-based proteins like beans or lentils, which need just a fraction of these resources. By choosing to reduce our meat intake, we directly save precious water resources—a benefit that's desperately needed in many parts of our world.

Embracing a diet that's less reliant on meat doesn't mean you must abandon it altogether, unless that aligns with your personal values. Start with manageable changes, like participating in Meatless Mondays. This one day each week without meat can tremendously reduce your carbon footprint over time. Research from Oxford University suggests that if everyone adopted a meat-free Monday, it would reduce greenhouse gas emissions by the equivalent of taking over 16 million cars off the road for a year. That's a phenomenal impact for such a simple action.

The health benefits of cutting down on meat are well-documented, contributing to lower risks of heart disease, stroke, diabetes, and certain cancers. Plant-based meals can be delicious, nutritious, and full of variety. Don't feel like you're giving something up; rather, think of it as gaining a new world of culinary experiences. Why not experiment with dishes from Mediterranean, Middle Eastern, or Southeast Asian cuisines that naturally incorporate a lot of plant-based ingredients? Your taste buds will thank you, and so will the planet.

Reducing meat consumption is also about rethinking the role of animal products in our daily lives. The modern factory farming system is not only resource-intensive but also raises significant ethical concerns. By opting for less meat, we're making a stand against these unsustainable and often inhumane practices. Support companies and farms that practice ethical and sustainable animal husbandry. If you do eat meat, choose options that are organically raised, free-range, and grass-fed.

Thinking more consciously about meat requires an understanding of where our food comes from and the ramifications of its production. The average meal travels thousands of miles before it lands on our plates, contributing to carbon emissions from transportation. Additionally, the energy involved in processing, packaging, and preserving meat further adds to its environmental impact. By reducing our meat intake and opting for locally sourced products, we cut down on this hidden transportation carbon footprint.

Sustainable eating isn't just for the affluent; it's achievable on any budget. Beans, lentils, chickpeas, and other legumes are not only cheaper than meat but also rich in protein and vital nutrients. What's more, they can be stored for long periods, reducing waste and saving money. Seasonal vegetables and fruits, often more affordable than out-of-season produce, offer exceptional flavor and nutrition. Explore your local farmers' markets or join a CSA (Community Supported Agriculture) program to get fresh, local, and often organic produce.

Community plays a pivotal role in fostering sustainable habits. Cooking plant-based meals together can be a wonderful social activity, strengthening bonds while spreading awareness. Schools, workplaces, and community centers can set up programs or challenges to encourage meat reduction. Initiatives like these make the journey less daunting and more collective, providing support and shared learning experiences.

Furthermore, educating ourselves and others about the environmental costs of meat consumption can create a ripple effect. Share articles, host discussions, or even organize cooking classes focused on plant-based recipes. Knowledge is empowering, and it can inspire others to make changes in their own lives. It's essential to approach these conversations with empathy and openness, as everyone is on their own journey toward sustainability.

Technology, too, offers assistance in this transition. Numerous apps can help you discover plant-based recipes, plan meals, and even find local restaurants that offer vegetarian and vegan options. Social media platforms abound with influencers and communities dedicated to sustainable eating. These resources can provide inspiration, practical tips, and a sense of connection with like-minded individuals.

Lastly, let's not forget about the broader impacts. Our food choices influence supply chains and market demands. By reducing meat consumption, we send a clear message to producers and retailers about the importance of sustainability. This can lead to more sustainable farming practices, increased availability of plant-based alternatives, and ultimately a shift towards a more balanced and environmentally friendly food system.

In conclusion, reducing meat consumption is a powerful and accessible way to contribute to environmental sustainability. It's a multifaceted approach that benefits not only the planet but also our health, our wallets, and our communities. Start small, stay committed, and celebrate the positive changes you're making. Every meal is an opportunity to align your values with your actions, creating a more sustainable future one bite at a time.

As we continue our journey through sustainable food choices, remember: Each step you take, no matter how small, brings us closer to a healthier planet. Let's embrace the challenge of reducing meat consumption with enthusiasm and creativity. The rewards for ourselves and the environment are immense and profoundly worth the effort.

Home Gardening

In a world where everything seems to be wrapped in plastic, neatly packaged, and far removed from its origin, home gardening offers a refreshing alternative. It's a return to basics, a hands-on connection to the food we consume, and a tangible way to practice sustainability. Not only does it provide you with fresh produce, but it also fosters a deeper appreciation for the environment.

But why, you may wonder, should we take up the spade and glove? The benefits of home gardening stretch far beyond the harvest. By growing your own vegetables and herbs, you'll reduce your reliance on industrial agriculture, which is often dependent on pesticides, herbicides, and fossil fuels. This simple act can significantly lower your carbon footprint.

Moreover, home gardening combats food wastage. When you grow your own food, you'll be more likely to consume it rather than letting it spoil in the back of your fridge. The process of nurturing a plant from seedling to sprout teaches valuable lessons in patience, responsibility, and the importance of resource conservation. The experience is a gentle reminder that food doesn't simply appear on supermarket shelves; it's cultivated with care.

Gardening also paves the way for a more mindful consumption pattern. Picture this: A sun-kissed tomato fresh off the vine tastes worlds apart from its store-bought counterpart. The flavors are more vibrant, and there's an immeasurable satisfaction that comes from eating something you grew yourself. Suddenly, that salad from your backyard bounty becomes a celebration of what nature offers.

To get started, you don't need a sprawling backyard. Urban dwellers can make the most of balconies, rooftops, and even window sills. Containers, raised beds, and vertical gardening techniques offer versatile solutions for limited space. It's about making the space work for you.

Begin with understanding your local climate and growing season. These factors dictate what you can grow and when. Research which plants thrive best in your region and start small. Herbs like basil, parsley, and thyme are low-maintenance and can be grown in pots on your kitchen window. Their presence will also invigorate your cooking with fresh flavors.

Soil health is the cornerstone of a successful home garden. Good soil fosters root strength, moisture retention, and nutrient availability. Composting at home, as discussed in the "Reducing Waste" chapter, plays a pivotal role here. By turning your organic waste into rich compost, you create a sustainable, nutrient-rich medium for your plants. It's a circular process that encapsulates the essence of sustainable living.

Water is another critical resource. Depending on your region, water conservation techniques might be necessary. Using rainwater barrels can help reduce dependency on municipal water and is especially beneficial for gardens. Mulching is also vital; it helps retain soil moisture and suppresses weed growth, reducing the need for frequent watering and weeding.

Remember, gardening isn't without its challenges. Pests, disease, and unpredictable weather can sometimes dampen efforts. But these obstacles often bring out the most ingenious and sustainable solutions. Think companion planting—where certain plants support each other's growth by deterring pests and enhancing soil nutrients. Marigolds, for instance, can keep nematodes at bay, and aromatic herbs may repel aphids. It's all about creating a mini-ecosystem that works in harmony.

As your garden flourishes, so will your connection with the earth, each plant a testament to your commitment to a sustainable lifestyle. You'll find that gardening isn't just a method of producing food but a meditative practice, grounding you in the rhythms of nature. When the air is thick with the scent of fresh herbs, and your hands bear the proof of honest work, the reward is immeasurable.

Of course, vegetable gardens aren't the only option. Fruit trees, berry bushes, and even medicinal plants can all play a part in a diversified home garden. If space allows, consider integrating these for a broader spectrum of homegrown produce. They'll offer year-round benefits as well as a delightful variety to your diet.

Connecting kids to home gardening can instill in them values of sustainability from a young age. Teaching them where food comes from and allowing them to take part in the growing process can spark lifelong passion and behavioral change. Plus, it's a productive way to get them off screens and into the natural world.

For those who want to dive even deeper, permaculture gardening provides a comprehensive approach to sustainable horticulture. It emphasizes the interconnectedness of plants, animals, and humans within the garden ecosystem. Techniques such as no-till farming, polycultures, and natural water management can transform a simple garden into a self-sustaining eco-friendly oasis.

In urban settings, community gardens offer an invaluable resource. They foster a sense of community, provide educational opportunities, and reclaim oft-neglected spaces for productive use. Whether you're new to gardening or an experienced green thumb, joining a community garden can amplify your impact and extend the benefits of home gardening to a larger audience.

Even if you start small with a single pot of basil on your window sill, every little bit helps. That's the beauty of home gardening; it's scalable, adaptable, and continuously rewarding. The more you invest in it, the more you get back—not just in tomatoes or cucumbers but in a deeper understanding and appreciation of our environment.

So, let your home garden be a testament to what sustainable food choices are all about. Enjoy the fresh produce, revel in the learning process, and know that with each seed you plant, you're taking a step toward a healthier planet. The time to start is now. Digging into the soil might just be the most profound way to not only feed yourself but also nourish the earth.

Chapter 6:
Water Conservation

Water conservation emerges as a pivotal practice that, when embraced, can ripple outward to enact substantial environmental change. Begin at home: subtle shifts like installing low-flow showerheads and fixing drippy faucets can collectively preserve gallons of water daily. If your area permits, consider implementing rainwater harvesting systems, which capture precious rainfall for garden hydration and non-potable uses. Xeriscaping, incorporating drought-resistant and native plants into your landscape, not only curbs water consumption but also supports local biodiversity. Each action, though seemingly minor, infuses our daily routines with purpose and helps safeguard one of our planet's most essential and finite resources.

Efficient Water Use in the Home

When it comes to water conservation, the home is a perfect place to start. Freshwater is a precious resource, and its scarcity is becoming an increasingly pressing issue worldwide. But there's tremendous power in collective small changes. In this section, we'll explore practical and actionable ways to make your home's water use more efficient, helping you save money and contribute to a sustainable future.

Often, the illusion of abundant water is easy to maintain because it flows so freely from our taps. Yet, those who are environmentally conscious know that every drop counts. Let's start with the most obvious place where we use water daily: the bathroom. Simple changes here can make a big difference.

Upgrading old fixtures is one of the most impactful steps you can take. Install low-flow showerheads, faucets, and toilets to drastically cut down on water usage without sacrificing performance. A low-flow showerhead can reduce water flow to about 2.5 gallons per minute or less, while still providing adequate pressure. Additionally, dual-flush toilets allow you to use a lower volume flush for liquid waste and a higher volume flush for solid waste, optimizing water use.

Another area to focus on is daily habits. Small actions like turning off the faucet while brushing your teeth or shaving can save significant amounts of water over time. Placing a bucket in the shower to catch water while it heats up can provide water for plants or cleaning purposes. These might seem like minor adjustments, but they can lead to substantial savings in water and utility costs.

Moving to the kitchen, it's surprisingly easy to make adjustments. For instance, washing dishes can consume a lot of water. When washing by hand, fill one side of the sink with soapy water and the other with rinse water instead of keeping the tap running. If you use a dishwasher, make sure it is fully loaded before running it. Modern, energy-efficient dishwashers often use less water than washing by hand, though it might vary by model and usage habits.

Consider your laundry habits as well. Wait until you have a full load before running the washing machine. If your machine has adjustable water levels, set it to the appropriate level for the size of your load. Alternatively, investing in a high-efficiency washer can reduce water usage significantly. These machines use less water per cycle and are designed to clean clothes effectively with lower volumes of water.

Let's not forget about leaks. Dripping faucets, running toilets, and other types of leaks can waste hundreds of gallons of water over time.

Regularly check your home for leaks and fix them as soon as possible. A small investment in some basic plumbing tools can help you handle minor repairs yourself, avoiding the need for professional services and further reducing water waste.

Gardening and outdoor spaces also offer significant opportunities for water conservation. Watering plants early in the morning or late in the evening minimizes water evaporation caused by the sun's heat. Use mulch around plants to retain soil moisture, and consider setting up a drip irrigation system that delivers water directly to the roots, where it's needed most.

Collecting rainwater can provide a sustainable water source for your garden. Simple rain barrels attached to downspouts can collect hundreds of gallons of water during the rainy season. This water can then be used for outdoor watering needs, reducing your reliance on municipal water supplies.

Beyond these tips, fostering a culture of mindfulness about water use within your household is key. Educate family members about the importance of water conservation and include them in the process. This ensures everyone is on the same page and working together towards more efficient water use.

Indoor plants can serve as natural humidifiers, reducing the need for mechanical systems that consume water. Choose houseplants that don't require frequent watering, and place saucers beneath plant pots to catch excess water that can be reused.

Green home improvements offer an excellent opportunity to integrate water-saving technologies into your home during renovations. Installing greywater systems is one such example. These systems recycle water from sinks, showers, and laundry for use in irrigation or toilet flushing, thus drastically reducing the amount of freshwater you consume daily.

The path to efficient water use in the home is paved with awareness and intention. By rethinking our daily habits, investing in water-saving technologies, and fostering a conservation mindset, we can make meaningful strides towards a more sustainable future. We'll discover that mindful water use not only conserves a precious resource but also enriches our lives by fostering a deeper connection with our environment.

Rainwater Harvesting

Rainwater harvesting is an age-old practice that offers a contemporary solution to some of our most pressing water conservation challenges. By capturing and storing rainwater, we can reduce our dependence on municipal water systems, cut down on water bills, and ensure a sustainable supply of water for various uses around the home. It's a straightforward yet profoundly impactful practice that anyone can adopt.

At its core, rainwater harvesting involves collecting rain that falls on rooftops, filtering it to remove debris, and storing it for later use. This water can be used for a variety of purposes ranging from irrigation and gardening to toilet flushing and even washing cars. In many parts of the world, it's also treated and used as a primary source of drinking water. Incorporating rainwater harvesting into your lifestyle is easier than you might think, and the benefits are substantial.

To start, you don't need a complex setup. Basic systems involve gutters, downspouts, and a collection barrel. For those aiming to maximize their collection and usage, more advanced systems can incorporate filters, pumps, and large storage tanks. Each setup can be tailored to fit the needs and spatial constraints of your home, making rainwater harvesting an adaptable practice regardless of your living situation.

The simplicity of a rain barrel system cannot be overstated. A rain barrel, typically a 55-gallon drum, is placed beneath a downspout to collect rainwater from the roof. The water can then be used directly from the barrel for things like watering garden plants. It's an incredibly effective way to make use of rainwater with minimal investment and effort.

For more advanced systems, *cisterns* can be utilized. These are larger storage containers, often positioned underground or above ground in discreet areas. Cisterns can store hundreds to thousands of gallons of water. Incorporating filtration systems ensures this water is clean and suitable for various domestic uses. This setup allows harvested rainwater to be used more comprehensively, including for indoor usage such as laundry or even potable water after appropriate treatment.

One of the most compelling reasons to adopt rainwater harvesting is its environmental impact. Think about the stress we place on municipal water supplies, especially in regions prone to drought. By using harvested rainwater for non-potable needs, we're alleviating a considerable burden. This practice reduces the energy and resources associated with treating and transporting tap water, resulting in a tangible environmental benefit.

Moreover, rainwater harvesting can help mitigate urban flooding. In cities, a significant amount of rainfall is diverted to storm drains, creating overflows and flooding issues. By capturing and using rainwater at the source, we can significantly reduce runoff, aiding in the prevention of localized flooding. This practice, when adopted widely, can create a remarkable shift in how urban landscapes manage water.

Investing in rainwater harvesting also provides a measure of self-sufficiency. Dependence on municipal water supplies renders households vulnerable to water shortages, rising water costs, and service disruptions. Harvesting rainwater can serve as a buffer against such issues, providing homeowners with a reliable backup.

Installing a rainwater harvesting system may seem like a daunting task, but numerous resources are available to guide you through the process. Many municipalities offer rebates and incentives to support the adoption of rainwater harvesting systems. Additionally, there are an abundance of online tutorials, workshops, and community groups dedicated to promoting this practice and offering hands-on assistance.

For those concerned about the initial costs, it's crucial to consider the long-term savings on water bills and the benefits to the environment. Initial investments in equipment and installation are often offset by the quick return on investments, especially in regions with high water costs or frequent water restrictions. Plus, the potential to combine rainwater harvesting with other sustainability practices, such as xeriscaping and using native plants, can amplify the benefits.

The holistic impact of rainwater harvesting extends beyond individual households. As more communities adopt these practices, we move collectively toward a more sustainable and resilient future. Imagine neighborhoods where rainwater is utilized effectively, reducing pressure on community water sources and fostering a sense of shared responsibility toward environmental stewardship.

To truly embrace water conservation, rainwater harvesting should be viewed as a fundamental practice. It aligns seamlessly with other sustainability efforts and offers practical, actionable steps toward making a real difference. By adopting rainwater harvesting, you're not just saving water; you're actively participating in safeguarding our planet's future. Every droplet captured is a step closer to creating a harmonious relationship with the natural world.

So, let's explore what it takes to integrate rainwater harvesting into our everyday lives. With the right resources, knowledge, and a bit of effort, we can make rainwater harvesting a natural part of our routine. It's a transformation that begins with understanding its value and culminates in seeing the tangible benefits it brings to our environment and our lives.

Xeriscaping and Native Plants

When it comes to water conservation, few strategies are as effective or visually appealing as xeriscaping. This method of landscaping eliminates the need for excessive irrigation by using drought-resistant plants and innovative design principles. But the true beauty of xeriscaping isn't just in its efficiency. It's also in its harmony with the natural environment, a promising way to maintain aesthetic appeal while conserving a precious resource.

Xeriscaping starts with a thoughtful plan. Effective xeriscaping hinges on the selection of plants that thrive with minimal water. These aren't your typical garden-variety greens. They are hardy, drought-tolerant species that have adapted to local conditions over millennia. Think succulents, ornamental grasses, and native wildflowers. By prioritizing these, you drastically reduce the demand for water and maintenance, creating a landscape that practically takes care of itself.

Another essential principle of xeriscaping is the use of native plants. Native species have evolved to thrive in your specific climate and soil, making them naturally resistant to local pests and weather fluctuations. This resilience means you won't need to rely on synthetic pesticides or fertilizers, which further cuts down on environmental impact. Imagine a garden that not only survives but flourishes through the hottest, driest months with little more than the rain that falls naturally. That's the magic of native plants in xeriscaping.

Incorporating native plants isn't merely about water conservation; it's also about fostering biodiversity. Native plants support local wildlife, including butterflies, bees, and birds. These creatures rely on indigenous flora for shelter and sustenance. By choosing to plant milkweed, goldenrod, or coneflower, you're creating a living sanctuary for pollinators and other beneficial species. This not only supports ecological health but also enriches the vibrancy and dynamics of your garden.

To achieve the full benefits of xeriscaping, consider integrating techniques like mulch and efficient irrigation systems. Mulch acts as a protective barrier, reducing water evaporation from the soil and suppressing weed growth, which means your plants get more of the moisture they need without competition. Drip irrigation, a low-pressure system that delivers water directly to the roots, can supplement natural rainfall with targeted hydration, ensuring no drop is wasted.

Xeriscaping is also about understanding and utilizing micro-climates within your garden. Different areas of your yard will receive varying amounts of sunlight and wind exposure. By mapping out these micro-climates, you can place your plants in locations where they'll thrive best—grouping sun-loving species together and giving shade-preferring plants their own cozy nooks. This thoughtful arrangement helps create a cohesive and resilient landscape.

One major advantage of xeriscaping is the freeing up of time. Traditional lawns and flower beds can be labor-intensive, requiring constant watering, mowing, and fertilizing. In contrast, a well-planned xeriscape practically runs itself. Once established, native plants need minimal intervention, allowing you to step back and enjoy your garden without the relentless upkeep. This can be particularly liberating for busy individuals looking to balance sustainability with other life commitments.

There's also an economic benefit to xeriscaping. Lower water bills are just the beginning. Reduced need for fertilizers, pesticides, and general maintenance tools means your ongoing costs drop significantly. Many municipalities offer tax incentives or rebates for xeriscaping, acknowledging its positive impact on public water supplies. These financial perks make the initial investment in a xeriscape garden all the more worthwhile.

In designing your xeriscape, aesthetics need not be sacrificed. With an array of textures, colors, and forms available through native plants, your garden can be a masterpiece of natural beauty. Think of the soft, silver leaves of lamb's ear against vibrant purple sage, the airy plumes of ornamental grasses beside the earthy tones of yucca. This diversity not only beautifies your space but also creates a dynamic environment that changes with the seasons, offering new sights and sensations year-round.

On the subject of trees, consider opting for those that are both native and drought-tolerant. Trees like oak, juniper, or pine provide essential shade, which can reduce the water requirements of nearby plants. Their deep root systems also help to stabilize soil and reduce erosion, contributing to the health of your landscape. A well-placed tree can even lower your home's air conditioning costs by providing natural cooling.

While xeriscaping heavily emphasizes native plants and reduced water usage, it doesn't mean you can't include some of your favorite non-native species. The key is integration and moderation. Use these plants as accents rather than focal points to limit their water consumption. Grouping them in high-visibility areas where you can easily cater to their needs without impacting the overall efficiency of your garden is a wise approach.

Transitioning to a xeriscape can be as gradual or immediate as you choose. Start small with a section of your yard, experimenting with different plant combinations and designs. This way, you can see firsthand how native plants and xeriscaping principles work in your specific conditions without feeling overwhelmed. With time, as you observe the benefits, you might find yourself inspired to expand this sustainable approach across your entire garden.

Xeriscaping offers more than just practical benefits; it aligns with a broader philosophy of living sustainably and harmoniously with our environment. It invites us to rethink traditional approaches to gardening and landscaping, to recognize the inherent wisdom in nature's design. By adopting xeriscaping, we embrace a practice that respects natural resources, nurtures local ecosystems, and creates a lasting legacy of beauty and resilience.

Lastly, let's not forget the role of community in fostering xeriscaping practices. Sharing knowledge, resources, and even seeds with neighbors can help spread the benefits. Community gardens and public spaces that employ xeriscaping principles serve as living examples of sustainable landscaping. By connecting with others who are passionate about conservation, you can amplify your impact, learning and growing together toward a greener future.

By opting for xeriscaping and native plants, you're making a conscientious choice that ripples outwards, promoting water conservation and ecological balance. It's a step toward a more sustainable, beautiful world—one garden at a time.

Chapter 7:
Green Home Improvements

R evamping your living space with green home improvements is not just an investment in your property—it's a commitment to the planet. Imagine using eco-friendly building materials that don't deplete natural resources, installing smart home technologies to optimize energy usage, and embracing sustainable interior design that enriches your surroundings while preserving the environment. By taking these steps, we create healthier, more efficient homes that align with our values of sustainability and mindful living. These changes might seem small, but collectively, they contribute to significant reductions in our ecological footprint. Start small or go big; either way, every improvement brings us closer to a truly sustainable home.

Eco-Friendly Building Materials

Transitioning a home into a green haven begins with the materials you choose. Not only do they contribute to a healthier living environment, but they also lessen the overall environmental impact. Eco-friendly building materials can be just as aesthetically pleasing and functional as conventional options, often surpassing them in innovation and sustainability. By opting for these materials, you're investing in a future that prioritizes the earth's well-being.

One of the key players in the realm of sustainable building materials is reclaimed wood. This material breathes new life into aged wood from old barns, factories, and even wine barrels. Not only does reclaimed wood offer a unique, rustic charm that new wood can't replicate, but it also reduces the demand for virgin timber and minimizes deforestation. Each piece carries its own history, adding character to any home improvement project.

Bamboo is another powerhouse in sustainable construction. Rapidly renewable, bamboo can grow up to several feet a day, making it an exceptionally sustainable alternative. Its ability to regenerate so quickly means that it puts considerably less strain on natural resources. Bamboo is incredibly versatile—utilized in flooring, cabinetry, and even furniture—bringing an elegant and modern touch to any space.

Recycled metal is yet another option worth considering. Often derived from industrial scraps or repurposed consumer goods, recycled metals can be used in roofing, plumbing, and structural supports. Metals like steel and aluminum can be recycled indefinitely without losing strength or durability. This practice not only reduces the demand for new raw materials but also lowers energy consumption during the production process.

Natural insulation options have been gaining traction as well. Materials such as sheep's wool, cellulose, and cork are excellent alternatives to conventional fiberglass insulation. Sheep's wool is naturally fire-resistant and effectively regulates moisture, preventing mold growth. Cellulose, often made from recycled newspaper, provides excellent thermal performance. Cork, harvested from the bark of cork oak trees, is both renewable and biodegradable, offering exceptional insulation capabilities.

Let's not forget about sustainable concrete alternatives like hempcrete and ferrock. Hempcrete is made from the inner fibers of the hemp plant mixed with lime, creating a lightweight, breathable material that's resistant to mold and pests. Ferrock, on the other hand, utilizes recycled steel dust and combines it with other materials to form a product that's even stronger than traditional concrete. Both hempcrete and ferrock drastically reduce the carbon footprint associated with building materials.

In the realm of interior design, eco-friendly options abound. Recycled glass countertops, for instance, offer a stunning and durable surface for kitchens and bathrooms. Made from repurposed glass bottles and other waste material, these countertops are not only beautiful but also represent a practical way to reduce landfill waste. Similarly, tiles made from recycled materials or sustainable ceramics can add both charm and sustainability to any room.

When considering paints and finishes, low-VOC (volatile organic compounds) and zero-VOC options are essential for maintaining indoor air quality. Traditional paints release harmful chemicals into the air, which can contribute to a range of health issues. Eco-friendly paints, however, avoid these risks, ensuring a healthier living environment. Brands focusing on natural pigments and sustainable practices provide a wide array of colors and finishes that don't compromise on aesthetics.

Sustainable textiles are another element worth integrating into your home. Organic cotton, linen, and hemp fabrics offer durability and comfort without the environmental downside of conventional cotton farming. Organic cotton, for example, eliminates the use of synthetic pesticides and fertilizers, which are harmful to both the ecosystem and human health. Hemp and linen are known for their minimal water requirements and rapid growth rates, thus posing a lower environmental impact.

Even the smallest details can make a big difference. Reclaimed or sustainably sourced hardware, like knobs and handles, can complement your eco-friendly design ethos. Repurposing vintage pieces or choosing items made from recycled materials can add a unique touch to your home while staying true to sustainable principles.

For those looking to build from the ground up, straw bale construction is an innovative and eco-friendly option. Straw bales, used as insulation within the walls, provide exceptional thermal performance and are a byproduct of the agricultural industry. They are biodegradable and have a low embodied energy, making them a remarkably sustainable building choice.

In recent years, there has been a surge in the popularity of rammed earth and cob construction techniques, both of which use natural materials to create sturdy and energy-efficient buildings. Rammed earth involves compacting a mixture of soil, sand, and clay into formwork to create solid walls, which are both aesthetically pleasing and thermally stable. Cob, a similar mixture of clay, sand, and straw, is sculpted by hand to create walls, giving a unique and organic look to the home.

Innovation in the field of eco-friendly building materials continues to grow, offering more options for sustainable construction now than ever before. Green roofs, for instance, provide environmental benefits by reducing stormwater runoff, improving air quality, and creating habitats for wildlife. These living roofs not only enhance the visual appeal of the home but also significantly contribute to energy efficiency by providing natural insulation.

Another modern innovation is the use of mycelium, the root structure of mushrooms, as a building material. Mycelium can be grown into virtually any shape, providing a versatile and sustainable alternative to traditional building materials. Not only is mycelium completely biodegradable, but it also has insulating properties and is resistant to fire and mold.

Incorporating eco-friendly building materials into your home improves personal health and well-being, reduces environmental impact, and supports the global shift towards sustainable living. Each choice you make in the construction or renovation process, no matter how small, contributes to a broader culture of sustainability and conservation. Embracing these green alternatives is not just a commitment to your immediate environment but an investment in the future of our planet.

By selecting materials with a lower environmental impact, we can reimagine our living spaces as places that harmonize with nature rather than deplete it. This shift towards sustainability begins with thoughtful, informed decisions and grows into a lifestyle that prioritizes the health of the earth and its inhabitants. As we continue to innovate, the possibilities for eco-friendly building materials are boundless, promising a greener, healthier future for all.

Smart Home Technologies

In the quest to make our homes greener and more sustainable, embracing smart home technologies is a game-changer. These advancements offer us the ability to monitor, control, and optimize energy consumption in ways never previously possible. By integrating smart devices, homeowners can achieve remarkable energy savings, reduce carbon emissions, and contribute significantly to environmental conservation.

Smart thermostats stand at the forefront of these technologies. Devices like the Nest Learning Thermostat or the Ecobee learn your routine and preferences to ensure your home is heated and cooled only when necessary. By automatically adjusting the temperature based on your habits, these thermostats can significantly cut down on energy use. Imagine the cumulative impact of every household setting their thermostat efficiently—both on their energy bills and the planet.

Lighting is another area where smart technology can make a big difference. Smart bulbs and lighting systems allow you to control lights remotely, schedule them to turn on or off at specific times, and even adjust the brightness or color to suit the time of day or activity. Philips

Hue and LIFX are popular examples. These systems use LED technology, which is already more energy-efficient than traditional bulbs, and take it a step further by eliminating energy waste.

Energy monitoring devices provide detailed insights into how much energy your home appliances are using. Systems such as Sense and the Emporia Vue help track energy consumption in real-time, identifying energy hogs and giving homeowners actionable data to make informed decisions. By knowing which devices consume the most energy, you can prioritize replacing older, less efficient appliances or change use patterns, making your household more efficient.

Smart plugs and power strips offer another way to cut down on so-called "phantom" energy use. These devices allow you to control the power supply to appliances that aren't in use but still draw power. With apps that can manage these remotely, you can ensure that energy is only flowing to devices that are active, slashing unnecessary energy expenditure.

One of the most promising advancements in smart home technology is in the realm of home automation systems. Companies like SmartThings and HomeKit provide platforms that can integrate various smart devices under a single app. This unified control system can automate multiple aspects of your home's operation, from lighting and heating to security systems and appliances, optimizing their usage and making it easy to maintain energy efficiency.

Similarly, smart home hubs or controllers can connect different smart devices within your home, creating a cohesive system that works together seamlessly. Amazon Echo, Google Home, and Apple HomePod act as centralized command centers for all your smart devices. This level of integration and control allows for more sophisticated setups, like having your thermostat lower, your blinds close, and your lights dim automatically as you leave home—all of which contribute to energy savings.

The integration of renewable energy sources with smart home technology is another frontier with immense potential. Solar panels equipped with smart inverters can effectively manage the energy flow, optimizing the usage of solar power and storing excess in home batteries for future use. By connecting these systems to smart home apps, homeowners get real-time data on energy production and consumption, enabling better energy management and reducing dependency on non-renewable energy sources.

Water conservation is a critical aspect of sustainability, and smart home technologies can play a substantial role here as well. Smart irrigation systems like Rachio or Orbit B-hyve Water Sprinkler Controllers adjust watering schedules based on local weather conditions and soil moisture levels, ensuring that water is used efficiently and only when necessary. Similar innovations in home plumbing systems can alert homeowners to leaks or areas of excessive water use, enabling prompt repairs and preventing water waste.

Smart home security systems contribute to sustainability by integrating with other smart home devices to optimize security measures without excessive energy use. For example, smart locks, cameras, and motion sensors can be programmed to work together, ensuring that security devices are only active when needed. Comprehensive security setups like Ring or ADT Smart Home can provide peace of mind while also being energy-efficient.

Voice assistants, like Amazon's Alexa, Google Assistant, and Apple's Siri, streamline the interaction with smart home technologies, making it easier than ever to control various devices through simple voice commands. These assistants can facilitate routines that encompass turning off lights, lowering the thermostat, or even managing appliance usage remotely, further reducing wasteful energy consumption.

The advent of smart kitchens is also a noteworthy trend in this domain. Innovations such as smart refrigerators, ovens, and dishwashers can help reduce energy and water consumption. Brands like Samsung and LG offer appliances that monitor usage patterns, suggest improvements, and even notify users of maintenance requirements. Refrigerators that keep track of food inventory and suggest recipes based on what's available can help minimize food waste, contributing to overall sustainability.

Incorporating smart window coverings like automated blinds and shades helps optimize natural light and thermal insulation, leading to less reliance on artificial lighting and heating. Brands such as Lutron and Somfy offer solutions that can be programmed to adjust based on the time of day and weather conditions, bringing another layer of efficiency to your home.

While the upfront investment in smart home technologies might seem daunting, the long-term benefits—both environmental and financial—are substantial. The reduction in energy and water bills, combined with decreased carbon emissions, makes the initial outlay worthwhile. Additionally, many governments and utility companies offer rebates or incentive programs for homeowners who adopt energy-efficient technologies, further offsetting the costs.

The adoption of smart home technologies also dovetails with the broader concept of the Internet of Things (IoT). As more devices connect and communicate with each other, the potential for optimizing energy use grows exponentially. With software updates and machine learning algorithms, these systems can improve over time, constantly refining their efficiency and offering new ways to save energy.

Moreover, by sharing data and insights with utility companies, smart home technologies can contribute to more efficient management of the power grid. This can reduce the need for excess power generation and help balance demand, benefiting the environment on a larger scale.

Smart home technologies are not merely about convenience; they represent a pivotal shift towards more responsible and sustainable living. By taking control of our energy consumption, automating systems for efficiency, and integrating renewable sources, we can significantly decrease our environmental impact. It's not just about reducing costs, but about fostering a more mindful, deliberate approach to how we use the resources available to us.

If every environmentally conscious individual invests in even a few smart devices, the collective impact can be immense. As with all aspects of sustainable living, the key is to start where you can and scale up gradually. Each small step contributes to a larger movement towards a healthier, more sustainable planet.

Sustainable Interior Design

Sustainable interior design isn't just about choosing the right materials; it's a way of life. A truly green home reflects not only the aesthetics but also the values of its occupants. When we think about sustainability in the fabric of our homes, it encompasses everything from the furniture we select to the paint on the walls, down to the smallest decor items. All these choices collectively reduce our environmental footprint and can contribute to a healthier living space.

First and foremost, consider how you furnish your home. Choosing second-hand or vintage furniture can be a great place to start. It's not only a sustainable choice but also a way to add unique character to your space. Older furniture often comes with a quality that's hard to find in new mass-produced items. If you're inclined towards new furniture, look for pieces made from FSC-certified wood or bamboo, which are both sustainable and durable.

Another crucial aspect is the use of non-toxic, eco-friendly materials. Indoor air quality can be significantly improved by choosing low-VOC (Volatile Organic Compounds) paints and finishes. Standard paints can release harmful chemicals into the air for years after application, impacting the health of your home's inhabitants. Select paints and finishes that are labeled as low-VOC or zero-VOC to ensure a healthier, safer environment.

When it comes to flooring, sustainable options abound. Reclaimed wood, cork, and bamboo are excellent choices. Reclaimed wood not only reduces the demand for new lumber but adds a rustic, timeless quality to your home. Cork is harvested from the bark of trees and can be done without harming the tree itself, making it another renewable resource. Bamboo, though technically a grass, mimics the look of wood and grows at an astonishing rate, making it a highly sustainable option.

Lighting is another key element in sustainable interior design. Natural light is, of course, the most eco-friendly. Maximize the use of windows and skylights to flood your spaces with daylight. For artificial lighting, opt for LED bulbs, which consume significantly less electricity and have a longer lifespan compared to traditional incandescent or even CFL bulbs. Additionally, consider using energy-efficient lighting fixtures and smart lighting systems that can be programmed or adjusted to reduce unnecessary energy use.

Textiles and fabrics also play a significant role. Choose organic cotton, linen, hemp, or recycled materials for your cushions, curtains, and rugs. These materials are not only sustainable but also free from the harmful pesticides and chemicals often used in conventional textile production. Furthermore, they tend to have a longer lifespan and better biodegradability.

Now, let's talk about decor. Incorporating elements of nature like indoor plants can enhance both the look and feel of your living spaces. Plants not only add a touch of greenery but also help to purify the air.

Opt for low-maintenance and air-purifying plants like spider plants, peace lilies, and snake plants. If you'd like to take it a notch higher, you can explore creating a living wall or a vertical garden inside your home.

Beyond aesthetics, consider multipurpose furniture. In urban settings where space is increasingly at a premium, pieces that serve more than one function can cut down on the need for additional items. For instance, a sofa bed, a dining table that doubles as a work-station, or a storage ottoman can be both practical and stylish solutions. This not only saves space but also reduces the resources spent manufacturing multiple pieces of furniture.

Repurposing and upcycling are other fantastic ways to integrate sustainability into your interior design. Transform an old ladder into a bookshelf or use wooden crates as wall-mounted storage units. The possibilities are endless when you let creativity guide your repurposing projects. Plus, these unique pieces often become conversation starters, adding a personal touch to your home.

When considering appliances and electronics, always look for Energy Star ratings or similar certifications. Energy-efficient appliances consume less electricity and water, helping to lower your utility bills and reduce your home's environmental impact. Moreover, some energy-efficient models come with smart technology that allows you to monitor and control your appliance use remotely, making it easier to operate them more sustainably.

Lastly, don't underestimate the impact of proper waste manag-ement. An organized home with well-segregated waste bins encourages recycling and composting, making it easier for everyone in the household to contribute to a zero-waste lifestyle. Consider placing recycling bins in convenient locations around your home, such as the kitchen and office spaces, to make it effortless to sort waste.

Implementing sustainable interior design practices doesn't have to happen overnight. Start by making small, conscious choices and gradually incorporate more eco-friendly options into your home. It's a journey worth taking, and every step you take contributes to a larger movement towards environmental conservation. By making sustainable choices in our living spaces, we set a powerful example for others and help shape a greener future.

Chapter 8:
Ethical Consumerism

As we navigate our daily lives, the choices we make as consumers have a tremendous impact on the environment. Ethical consumerism isn't just about picking products with green labels; it's about cultivating a mindful approach to every purchase, reflecting our values of sustainability and fairness. From scrutinizing brands for their ethical practices to understanding the devastating impact of fast fashion, our spending can support a more equitable and eco-friendly world. Simple habits like choosing quality over quantity, prioritizing reuse, and supporting local, ethical businesses can reduce waste and promote a more sustainable living model. By re-examining our habits and making informed choices, we can drive positive change, showing that each decision counts in the broader quest for a greener and more just planet.

Choosing Sustainable Brands

When embarking on the journey of ethical consumerism, selecting sustainable brands is a fundamental step. But what does it mean for a brand to be sustainable? Simply put, it's about ensuring that the brand's products, processes, and policies are aligned with environmental conservation and ethical responsibility. As consumers, we wield the power to drive significant change through our purchasing choices. The complexity of these decisions may seem daunting, but with a little guidance, you can make informed choices that align with your values.

Firstly, it's crucial to recognize that not all brands claiming sustainability live up to their promises. Greenwashing, a deceptive practice where companies exaggerate or fabricate their environmental efforts, is rampant. This makes it necessary to dig deeper than surface-level claims. Look for third-party certifications such as Fair Trade, B Corp, USDA Organic, and Cradle to Cradle. These certifications provide a level of assurance that the brand meets rigorous standards for social and environmental performance.

Transparency is another hallmark of a genuinely sustainable brand. Companies that are open about their supply chains, sourcing practices, and environmental impact are generally more trustworthy. Brands that publish annual sustainability reports and set clear, measurable goals for reducing their footprint are demonstrating accountability. For instance, brands that source materials responsibly and provide details on their labor conditions are usually more committed to ethical practices. Transparency builds credibility and helps you make more informed decisions.

Understanding the lifecycle of the products you purchase is also important. From raw material extraction to manufacturing, packaging, distribution, and disposal, each stage has an environmental impact. Aim to support brands that focus on circular economy principles— those that design products with longevity in mind, use recyclable or biodegradable materials, and have systems in place for product take-back and recycling. Such companies prioritize reducing waste and resource consumption throughout the product's lifecycle.

One compelling reason to choose sustainable brands is their commitment to innovation and quality. Sustainable brands often invest heavily in research and development to create eco-friendly alternatives to traditional products. Whether it's innovative materials like mushroom leather or waterless dyeing technologies, these advancements not only minimize environmental impact but also often lead to higher quality, longer-lasting products. As a consumer, you can feel good knowing that you're supporting pioneering efforts that pave the way for a more sustainable future.

Local and small-scale artisans also play a crucial role in the sustainable brand ecosystem. By sourcing products from local businesses, you not only reduce the carbon footprint associated with long-distance shipping but also support local economies. These small businesses often employ more sustainable methods, like handmade production techniques that require less energy. Moreover, local artisans are frequently more attuned to regional environmental and social issues, making their products more tailored to local sustainability needs.

Let's not overlook the influence of community and peer recommendations. Word-of-mouth, social media reviews, and sustainability-focused online communities are excellent resources. Sharing experiences with like-minded individuals can provide honest insights and recommendations. Trusted bloggers and influencers who emphasize transparency offer another layer of assurance. Their authentic reviews can guide you toward brands that truly make a difference.

Empathy and ethical considerations are at the heart of choosing sustainable brands. Companies that prioritize fair labor practices, humane working conditions, and equitable wages invest in the well-being of their workers and their communities. By choosing such brands, you support a more just and equitable global economy. Additionally, many sustainable brands give back through initiatives like tree planting, educational programs, or community development projects, amplifying the positive impact of your purchase.

Cost is often a concern when choosing sustainable brands. While these products may sometimes come with a higher price tag, it's essential to consider the true cost of cheaper alternatives. Fast fashion and low-cost goods often come at the expense of environmental degradation and poor labor conditions. By investing in sustainably made products, you're contributing to a system that values and respects natural and human resources. The notion of quality over quantity becomes paramount; fewer, better-made items can lead to more meaningful, long-term satisfaction.

Another strategy is to participate in or support platforms that facilitate ethical shopping. Websites and apps tailored to sustainable shopping offer curated lists of vetted brands and products, making it easier to navigate the ethical marketplace. Some platforms even provide reward systems or incentives for choosing sustainable options.

Additionally, consider your interaction with sustainable brands as an evolving journey. It's unlikely that any brand will be perfect, but incremental improvements are worth supporting. Engage with brands on social media to ask questions and hold them accountable for their claims. Your inquiries can spark dialogue and push companies to be more transparent and responsible.

The power of collective action cannot be understated. By making deliberate choices and supporting sustainable brands, you join a movement that demands better from our industries. This collective consumer power influences market trends and fosters a more profound cultural shift toward sustainability. When more people choose eco-friendly brands, it signals to larger corporations that there's a significant market demand for ethical practices, prompting broader transformations in business operations.

As you integrate these considerations into your purchasing habits, remember that every little step counts. Each sustainable choice contributes to a larger tapestry of environmental stewardship and ethical consumption. Your conscious decisions not only nurture the planet but also inspire others to follow suit. Small, consistent actions, when multiplied, drive monumental change.

Ultimately, ethical consumerism and choosing sustainable brands are acts of stewardship and care. They embody a conscious acknowledgment of our interconnectedness with the world. As you continue on this path, seek out brands that resonate with your values and foster a deeper connection to the environment and community. Embrace the journey, celebrate your progress, and remain steadfast in your commitment to sustainability.

Choosing sustainable brands isn't just a trend; it's a lifestyle. It requires mindfulness, informed decisions, and a willingness to explore and learn. By investing in companies that honor people and the planet, you're casting a vote for a healthier, more equitable world. And in doing so, you become an integral part of the solution—a champion for a brighter, greener future.

The Impact of Fast Fashion

Fashion has always been a way for us to express individuality, but the rise of fast fashion has transformed this expression into an environmental dilemma. Fast fashion refers to the rapid production of inexpensive clothing that emulates current trends. While it allows consumers to cycle through styles quickly, it comes at both an environmental and ethical cost.

The appeal of fast fashion is undeniable: brands churn out new "collections" every few weeks, enticing customers with the latest trends at rock-bottom prices. It's hard to resist a $5 T-shirt when it's labeled as the season's must-have. However, what lies beneath this shiny facade is a grim reality. From water pollution to labor exploitation, the consequences of fast fashion are profound and far-reaching.

The production process itself is resource-intensive. Clothing manufacturing is one of the largest polluters of freshwater in the world. Dyeing fabrics often involves toxic chemicals that seep into rivers and streams, affecting aquatic life and the communities that rely on these water sources. In places like Bangladesh and India, where many fast fashion factories are located, rivers have turned various hues from the runoff, making clean water a luxury rather than a necessity.

Moreover, the environmental impact extends beyond just pollution. Fast fashion thrives on the exploitation of labor in developing countries. Workers are paid minimal wages and often work in unsafe conditions. The 2013 Rana Plaza disaster is a haunting reminder of the human cost behind our affordable clothes. More than 1,100 workers perished when the factory complex collapsed, highlighting the negligence towards worker safety often ignored in the pursuit of profit.

Then there's the issue of waste. Fast fashion items are designed to be disposable. They're made quickly and cheaply, leading to garments that fall apart after just a few wears. This "wear it once" philosophy results in an extraordinary amount of textile waste. The average American throws away approximately 81 pounds of clothing each year, much of which ends up in landfills where synthetic fibers can take hundreds of years to decompose.

With all this in mind, it's clear that the seemingly harmless act of shopping can have a ripple effect on the environment and society. But what can be done to counteract this trend? The answer lies in embracing ethical consumerism. We need to shift our focus from quantity to quality, choosing garments that are made to last and crafted under fair labor practices. Supporting brands committed to sustainability means voting with your wallet and showing that there is a demand for change.

Consider the lifecycle of your clothing. Sustainable fashion advocates suggest buying less but opting for higher quality. Instead of purchasing five cheaply made shirts, invest in one or two well-crafted pieces from ethical brands. Not only will these items serve you longer, but they also often come with stories of artisanship and ecological mindfulness.

Additionally, being mindful about how we dispose of clothing is crucial. Instead of trashing that worn-out shirt, think about recycling or repurposing it. Many brands now offer recycling programs where you can drop off old garments in exchange for discounts on future purchases. This approach not only reduces landfill waste, but it also fosters a culture of reuse and repurpose.

Education is another vital component. Awareness campaigns and documentaries can shed light on the behind-the-scenes workings of the fast fashion industry. The more informed we are about the origins and impacts of our clothes, the better choices we can make. Schools, community groups, and social media platforms have significant roles to play in spreading this crucial information.

Engage in community initiatives that promote sustainable fashion. Clothing swaps are excellent ways to refresh your wardrobe without buying new items. At these events, you can exchange your pre-loved clothing for 'new-to-you' pieces. Not only does this save money, but it also reduces the demand for new products and builds a sense of community. Likewise, thrift stores and consignment shops offer avenues to give garments a second life and a second chance at making someone else happy.

Ultimately, breaking the cycle of fast fashion requires a cultural shift. It means redefining what it means to be "in style" by favoring timeless, high-quality pieces over fleeting trends. It's about valuing craftsmanship and sustainability over convenience and cost. It's about changing our mindset, focusing on needs over wants, and recognizing that every purchase we make casts a vote for the kind of world we want to live in.

The path to sustainable fashion isn't devoid of fun or style. Instead, it's a journey to discovering meaningful, unique pieces that tell a story and reflect personal values. As environmentally conscious individuals, we have the power to drive this change. We can create a future where fashion respects both the planet and the people who inhabit it.

The environmental and societal implications of fast fashion are severe, but they're not irreversible. By aligning our shopping habits with our ethical values, we can make significant strides toward a more sustainable world. It's about taking small, impactful steps—choosing quality over quantity, supporting ethical brands, recycling, reusing, and above all, staying informed. We each have an opportunity to turn the tide, making fashion a force for good instead of a contributor to environmental degradation and human suffering.

Mindful Shopping Habits

In today's consumer-driven world, mindful shopping habits offer a path to more environmentally conscious living. Many of us shop out of habit or convenience, often without considering the broader implications of our purchases. Becoming a mindful shopper means taking a step back, evaluating your needs versus your wants, and making choices that align with your values and the health of the planet.

Firstly, it's crucial to define what mindful shopping entails. It's not just about buying fewer things, although that certainly helps. It's about making deliberate choices that minimize harm to the environment and support ethical labor practices. When you practice mindful shopping, you're not just a consumer; you're an advocate for a better world.

To start, awareness is key. Look into the lifecycle of the products you buy. This includes how they're made, how they're packaged, and what happens to them after they're no longer useful. Take clothing as an example. Fast fashion might be cheap and trendy, but its environmental cost is high. Instead, invest in high-quality pieces that will last longer. Classic styles rarely go out of fashion and are often better made, reducing the frequency with which you need to replace them.

Another vital aspect of mindful shopping is considering the materials used in the products you buy. Opt for items made from sustainable materials, such as organic cotton, bamboo, or recycled fabrics. These materials have a lower environmental impact and often come from companies that prioritize sustainability.

However, mindful shopping isn't just about what you buy; it's about how you buy it. When possible, support local businesses rather than big-box stores. Local businesses often have smaller carbon footprints since their goods don't need to be transported over long distances. Plus, they contribute to the local economy and promote community well-being.

One might argue that it's difficult to verify the sustainability claims of brands. This is where third-party certifications can be incredibly useful. Certifications such as Fair Trade, USDA Organic, and Energy Star can guide you toward more ethical choices. These labels indicate that the product meets certain environmental and social standards, helping you make informed decisions without needing a deep dive into every purchase.

It's not only about new purchases. Consider the pre-owned market as well. Thrift stores, online resale platforms, and community swap events are excellent ways to find what you need without contributing to the demand for new production. Used items can often be just as good as new, especially if you're diligent about checking their condition before buying.

Think small, too. Even everyday items like household cleaners and personal care products offer opportunities for making a difference. Opt for eco-friendly, non-toxic products, which are not only better for the environment but often safer for your health as well. Making your own cleaning products with simple ingredients like vinegar and baking soda can also be a rewarding and sustainable practice.

In addition to what you buy, reflect on how much you buy. We live in a culture that often equates more with better, but this mindset contributes to waste and unnecessary production. Adopting a minimalist approach can lead to more thoughtful consumption. Before purchasing, ask yourself if you truly need the item or if it's something that will end up unused or forgotten.

Mindful shopping also intersects with reducing waste. A conscious consumer strives to minimize packaging waste by choosing products with less or more sustainable packaging. For example, buying in bulk can reduce the amount of plastic and cardboard you bring into your home. Reusable bags, containers, and produce bags can significantly cut down on single-use plastics.

Impulse buying can be another hurdle to mindful shopping. We've all been there, grabbing an item impulsively because it's on sale or catches our eye. One effective strategy to combat this is to implement a "24-hour rule." If you find something you want, wait a day before purchasing it. This cooling-off period helps you determine if the item is a necessity or just a fleeting desire.

It's also helpful to create a shopping list and stick to it. This not only helps prevent impulse buys but also allows for planned, thoughtful purchases. A well-considered list can be a tool for staying organized, budgeting effectively, and ensuring that your selections meet your needs.

Finally, education plays a crucial role in maintaining mindful shopping habits. Stay informed about the companies you buy from and their practices. Many brands offer transparency reports detailing their sustainability efforts. Engaging with these resources empowers you to make informed choices and supports companies that share your values.

In conclusion, adopting mindful shopping habits is an ongoing learning process that requires intention and effort. It's about making choices that reflect not just personal needs but also a broader commitment to environmental stewardship and social responsibility. Each mindful purchase is a vote for the kind of world you want to live in—one where sustainability and ethics take precedence. As you continue on this journey, remember that every choice, no matter how small, contributes to a larger impact.

Chapter 9:
Community Involvement

Taking individual steps toward sustainability is commendable, but when communities unite for a common environmental cause, the impact multiplies. Imagine the ripple effect created when local environmental initiatives gain momentum; small shifts can lead to significant change. Whether you're planting a community garden, participating in local clean-ups, or setting up educational workshops, your efforts can inspire others to join in. Volunteering opens up avenues to share resources, learn from others, and build a support network dedicated to green goals. By fostering a sense of community around sustainable living, we not only enhance our local environment, but also create a blueprint for broader societal change. Let's harness the power of community to amplify our efforts and create a lasting, positive influence on our planet.

Local Environmental Initiatives

Localized environmental efforts play an essential role in the global fight against climate change and environmental degradation. They bridge the gap between individual actions and broader, systemic changes. These initiatives not only reduce the ecological footprint of the community but also foster a collective sense of responsibility and empowerment.

In many towns and cities, community gardens have sprouted as a robust response to the growing concern for sustainable food sources.

These gardens offer more than just fresh produce; they act as educational hubs where members can learn about organic farming practices, composting, and the importance of pollinator habitats. It's a beautiful sight to see children and adults tending to crops side by side, connecting with the earth and each other. Beyond food production, these gardens contribute to urban greening, improving air quality and providing shade and aesthetic beauty in concrete jungles.

Cities also engage in tree-planting campaigns to enhance their green cover. Trees act as carbon sinks, improve air quality, and provide a cooling effect, which is particularly crucial in combating urban heat islands. By organizing tree-planting drives, communities can come together to plant saplings during weekends, ensuring that the growth and care of these trees become a shared, ongoing responsibility. Involving local schools, businesses, and residents creates a sense of ownership and pride, making it more likely for people to take proactive steps in nurturing their environment.

Many municipalities have adopted zero-waste policies, enacting aggressive recycling programs and waste reduction campaigns. These initiatives often include providing educational workshops on waste segregation, DIY recycling projects, and the importance of minimizing single-use plastics. Community-driven thrift shops or swap meets allow residents to exchange items, promoting the reuse of goods and reducing the overall consumption footprint. It's a practical step towards fostering a culture of mindful consumption and responsible waste management that leaves a lasting impact on future generations.

Another local initiative gaining traction is the establishment of repair cafes. These are community events where volunteers with various expertise offer free repair services for household items, from electronics to clothing. Not only does this reduce the number of items heading to landfills, but it also revives the culture of repairing and reusing rather than discarding and replacing. These cafes serve as informal learning centers where skills are shared, and a sense of self-reliance is cultivated, proving that sustainable living can be both practical and economically beneficial.

Beyond material goods, several towns are investing in renewable energy cooperatives. These co-ops enable residents to collectively fund and manage renewable energy projects such as solar panels or wind turbines. By producing clean energy locally, these communities reduce their dependency on fossil fuels and build resilience against energy price volatility. The cooperative model ensures that benefits are shared equitably among participants, fostering solidarity and a collective sense of achievement in reducing carbon emissions.

Local governments play a pivotal role by implementing policies that encourage sustainable practices. For instance, cities may introduce incentives for businesses and homes that integrate eco-friendly technologies such as rainwater harvesting systems, green roofs, and energy-efficient appliances. Some towns have even created green zones where only electric or hybrid vehicles are permitted, reducing air pollution and encouraging the adoption of cleaner transportation modes.

Public education campaigns are crucial in underpinning these local efforts. By raising awareness through town hall meetings, social media, public service announcements, and school curricula, communities can galvanize support for environmental initiatives. Information about sustainability practices and the particular challenges faced by the community can empower residents with the knowledge necessary to make significant changes in their daily lives. When people understand the direct consequences of their actions on their immediate environment, they are more likely to participate actively in conservation efforts.

Local environmental initiatives often extend to conservation and restoration projects, including the protection of local waterways, wetlands, and wildlife habitats. By organizing cleanup drives, citizen science projects, and habitat restoration activities, communities contribute to preserving the biodiversity essential for ecological balance. Volunteers removing invasive species or planting native vegetation can see, firsthand, the positive effects of their actions on local ecosystems.

Communities have also been leveraging technology to monitor and report environmental issues. Apps and platforms allow residents to track pollution levels, report illegal dumping, or participate in citizen science projects. This real-time data collection facilitates swift responses to environmental threats and ensures that local authorities are held accountable for maintaining environmental standards.

Schools and universities can serve as beacons of sustainability. Many educational institutions have adopted green practices, such as installing solar panels, creating recycling programs, and maintaining green roofs and gardens. By involving students in these projects, schools not only reduce their environmental impacts but also instill sustainable values in the next generation. These young people grow up understanding the importance of stewardship and are more likely to carry these values forward into their adult lives.

Let's not overlook the vital role of local businesses in these initiatives. Many small businesses have embraced sustainability by sourcing local and eco-friendly products, reducing waste, and employing green practices in their operations. These businesses often collaborate with local governments and NGOs to host eco-events, create awareness, and encourage responsible consumer behaviors among their patrons. Supporting these businesses sends a powerful message that sustainability is not just a buzzword, but a valued commitment within the community.

Every community has unique environmental challenges and strengths. By tailoring initiatives to match their specific needs and resources, communities can create more effective and sustainable solutions. The impact of these local efforts can ripple outwards, inspiring neighboring areas to take similar actions and contributing to a larger collective movement towards a greener future.

Local environmental initiatives embody the essence of grassroots activism. They remind us that while individual choices matter, the most significant changes often come from community-led efforts. When people unite with a common purpose, they not only transform their surroundings but also build a sense of belonging and shared responsibility. The journey to a sustainable future starts right where we are—in our neighborhoods, schools, parks, and local shops. Through these collective efforts, every small step becomes a giant leap towards a healthier planet.

Volunteer Opportunities

Engaging in volunteer opportunities is a pivotal way to merge personal passions with community needs, and for those of us who are environmentally conscious, it offers a tangible way to make an impact. Volunteering in environmental projects not only allows you to contribute to conservation efforts but also connects you with like-minded individuals. It can feel incredibly rewarding to see the direct results of your efforts, be it in cleaner parks, restored native habitats, or increased environmental awareness in your community.

Many organizations focus on environmental conservation and sustainability, and they often welcome volunteers with open arms. Whether you have a few hours to spare on a weekend or are seeking a more long-term commitment, there's likely a project that fits into your schedule. Local parks and nature reserves frequently need volunteers for activities such as habitat restoration, trail maintenance, and educational outreach. These hands-on projects not only protect and enhance natural settings but also foster a deeper connection with your local ecosystem.

Educational programs, especially those aimed at children and young adults, are another area where volunteers can make a significant impact. By participating in or organizing workshops, field trips, or even simple classroom presentations, you can inspire the next generation to take up the mantle of environmental stewardship. Teaching others about the importance of recycling, energy conservation, and sustainable living practices can create a ripple effect that extends far beyond your immediate efforts.

Beach and river cleanups are classic volunteer activities that offer immediate and visible results. Removing plastic and other pollutants from these vital habitats can significantly improve local wildlife health and enhance natural beauty. Such events are often organized by environmental nonprofits, local governments, or community groups, and they serve as a community rallying point around a shared cause. Participating in these cleanups also provides a powerful visual reminder of the importance of reducing our plastic usage and properly disposing of waste.

Community gardens and urban farming initiatives offer another fertile ground for volunteerism. These projects not only bring greenery and fresh produce to urban environments but also encourage sustainable agriculture practices. Volunteers here might engage in planting, weeding, composting, and even organizing educational events for residents. Beyond the environmental benefits, community gardens have the added advantage of fostering social connections and resilience among neighbors.

Citizen science projects provide a unique way to contribute to scientific understanding and environmental protection. These projects often involve gathering data on local wildlife, plant species, weather patterns, or pollution levels. By volunteering with citizen science initiatives, you can help researchers gather valuable data that informs conservation strategies and policy decisions. Participation in such projects not only benefits the environment but also enhances your knowledge and sharpen your observational skills.

Encouragingly, digital volunteering opportunities are on the rise. For those who may have physical limitations or prefer to contribute from the comfort of their home, there are many ways to get involved. This could include tasks like transcribing field notes for conservation projects, analyzing photos from wildlife cameras, or even helping with social media advocacy for environmental groups. This new form of volunteerism leverages technology to overcome geographical and physical barriers, allowing more people to contribute to environmental efforts.

Another area where you can significantly contribute is in advocacy and policy work. While grassroots efforts are crucial, systemic change often requires shifts in policy and legislation. Volunteering for advocacy groups can involve activities like writing to your local representatives, organizing or participating in rallies, and spreading awareness about pivotal environmental issues. Efforts in advocacy may seem abstract compared to hands-on work, but the potential for large-scale impact is immense.

Wildlife rehabilitation centers often welcome volunteers to help care for injured or orphaned animals. Tasks here can range from cleaning enclosures and preparing food to assisting with medical procedures and public education. Working with wildlife offers a unique and enriching way to contribute to conservation, and it provides a deeper appreciation of the species we coexist with.

Before jumping into a volunteer opportunity, it's beneficial to take a moment to consider where your skills and interests align. This reflection not only ensures that you enjoy and commit to the activity but also helps organizations place you in roles where you can be most effective. Whether your talents lie in organizing events, manual labor, public speaking, or scientific observation, there's a niche for you in the world of environmental volunteerism.

In addition to traditional volunteering, consider how your professional skills can contribute to environmental causes. For instance, graphic designers could help create educational materials, writers might assist in crafting compelling grant applications or awareness campaigns, and accountants could support nonprofits with financial planning. Utilizing your professional skills in a volunteer capacity can be highly fulfilling and also critical for the success of environmental initiatives.

By involving yourself in volunteer opportunities, you not only contribute to the immediate well-being of your community and environment but also become part of a broader movement towards sustainability. You help set a precedent for others, demonstrating that individual actions, when combined with community efforts, have the power to initiate significant change. It's about planting seeds—both literally and figuratively—towards a greener, more sustainable future.

One of the most inspiring aspects of volunteering is witnessing the collective impact of small actions. A single person planting a tree or cleaning up a section of beach might seem insignificant, but when multiplied by hundreds or thousands of volunteers, the results are extraordinary. This shared effort fuels momentum, making large-scale environmental goals seem more achievable.

Ultimately, volunteering serves as a bridge between individual lifestyle choices and collective community action. It's essential for those passionate about sustainability to consider how their time and efforts can ripple outwards. Whether you're digging in the dirt, educating a classroom, or advocating for policy change, your contributions matter. They matter to your community, to the environment, and to the generations that will inherit the Earth. So, let's roll up our sleeves and get to work because the planet needs us now more than ever.

Building a Green Community

In the transformative journey toward environmental conservation, individual actions undeniably carry weight. But imagine multiplying your efforts exponentially by involving your community. That's the power of building a green community. Together, we can create ripples of change that lead to a wave of sustainable living. Community involvement is the cornerstone of a long-lasting environmental impact. It's not just about reducing our footprints but about creating a collective path toward a greener future.

So, where do we start? The foundation of any green community lies in education and awareness. When people understand the why and how of sustainability, they are more likely to take meaningful action. Conduct workshops, host informational sessions, or organize local meetups with sustainability experts. The goal is to foster an environment where knowledge is freely shared and passed along. Not everyone's expertise needs to be planetary quantum physics; sometimes, it's those small, digestible nuggets of information that initiate the most change.

Inspiration Begets Action

Human beings are naturally inspired by stories and real-life examples. Highlight the efforts of local heroes who've made strides in sustainable practices. Whether it's a family that has successfully transitioned to a zero-waste lifestyle or a small business that employs green technologies, these stories serve as proof that sustainable living is achievable and beneficial. When community members see their neighbors achieving these goals, they will be more inclined to believe that they, too, can make a difference.

Another effective strategy is community challenges. Setting collective goals, such as reducing neighborhood waste by 20% over six months, can motivate everyone to participate. It's not just about the end goal; the journey fosters a stronger sense of community and shared responsibility. Acting together cultivates a supportive environment where successes are celebrated, and challenges are collectively overcome. Remember to use social media and local news outlets to share your milestones and victories. Public visibility can inspire others in your community and beyond.

Programs like community gardens offer another strong stepping stone toward building a green community. Imagine transforming a vacant lot into a thriving hub of local produce, where people can come together to learn about organic farming, reduce their carbon footprint, and nourish their families with fresh, local food. Community gardens aren't just about growing plants; they grow relationships and a collective sense of purpose. Local governments and organizations often provide grants or support to get these initiatives off the ground, so do a bit of homework and reach out. You'll be surprised at the resources available.

Shared Resources and Support Systems

A green community thrives on the principle of shared resources and support systems. Carpooling networks, tool libraries, and swap meets are practical ways to reduce waste and energy consumption while fostering a sense of community. Imagine borrowing a high-quality, seldom-used item like a power drill from a community tool library instead of each household purchasing one. These practices not only minimize waste but also promote a culture of sharing and collaboration.

Modern technology offers many ways to support these initiatives. Apps and social media platforms can connect members, coordinate events, and share resources efficiently. Whether it's a neighborhood

Facebook group or a dedicated community app, digital tools provide a quick and easy way to mobilize efforts. \'7bRemember, the more accessible you make sustainable practices, the more participation you'll garner.\'7d

Take, for instance, energy consumption. Why not share solutions for energy-efficient homes within your community? Organize tours of homes that have successfully implemented renewable energy sources or enhanced insulation and weatherproofing. These real-world examples offer practical insights and foster a network of mutual support where people share tips and pitfalls alike. It's all about creating a culture where eco-friendly living isn't seen as a chore but as a shared adventure, complete with communal benefits.

Engaging Local Governments and Businesses

A significant part of building a green community involves engaging local authorities and businesses. Start by advocating for greener policies and infrastructure in your town or city. Attend city council meetings, start petitions, and encourage others to do the same. Collective voices are harder to ignore. Push for more bike lanes, better public transit systems, and increased green spaces. Your local government has the power to make substantial structural changes that can significantly impact community sustainability.

Similarly, local businesses and corporations play a crucial role. Encourage them to adopt sustainable practices such as reducing plastic use, sourcing organic and local products, and supporting environmental initiatives. Start by supporting businesses already making eco-friendly choices and make your preferences known. Build relationships and open dialogues instead of confrontations. Many businesses would be open to making changes if they see a clear demand from their community. Partnerships between businesses, local government, and residents can lead to larger-scale projects like solar-powered community centers or neighborhood-wide recycling programs.

Nurturing the Next Generation

The responsibility of building a green community doesn't rest solely on current generations. It's essential to involve the younger members of the community in these efforts. Schools, youth groups, and educational programs can serve as excellent platforms for teaching sustainability. Incorporate environmental education into the curriculum and offer hands-on projects that allow kids to engage with sustainability directly. Imagine students learning about composting by managing their school garden or understanding energy efficiency through a local solar panel project.

When children and teenagers grow up with a solid understanding of environmental issues and sustainable practices, they're more likely to continue these efforts into adulthood. They also bring fresh perspectives and can be incredibly effective in influencing their families and peers toward greener choices.

In conclusion, building a green community is an ongoing, multifaceted effort that combines education, inspiration, shared resources, governmental and business engagement, and youth involvement. It's about creating a supportive network where everyone feels empowered to contribute and make a difference. You'll find that the collective benefits—stronger community bonds, improved local environment, and a heightened sense of purpose—are well worth the effort.

Chapter 10:
Eco-Friendly Travel

As we venture into the realm of eco-friendly travel, it's important to remember that our choices on the road can have a profound impact on the environment. Whether exploring local wonders or far-off places, adopting sustainable tourism practices helps preserve the beauty and cultural heritage of our destinations. Opt for accommodations that prioritize energy efficiency and waste reduction; many eco-lodges and green hotels provide comfortable and responsible options. Seek out low-impact travel destinations that have been recognized for their conservation efforts, and immerse yourself in the natural landscape while supporting locales committed to sustainability. Packing light and smart is crucial: it reduces the carbon footprint of your journey and simplifies your travels. Embrace reusable items such as water bottles, cloth bags, and eco-friendly toiletries. This chapter will guide you on how to integrate these practices seamlessly into your travel ethos, transforming every trip into a step forward for our planet.

Sustainable Tourism Practices

Traveling opens up new horizons and expands our understanding of the world. But with travel's profound joys comes a crucial responsibility: to ensure our journeys don't harm the very places we love to visit. Sustainable tourism encompasses a variety of practices aimed at minimizing the negative impacts of travel while maximizing its positive contributions to the environment, economy, and local communities.

Sustainable tourism starts even before you board a plane. The choices we make when planning our trips—like selecting eco-friendly accommodations and committing to travel during off-peak seasons—can drastically reduce our environmental footprint. Opt for accommodations that prioritize sustainability through energy-efficient systems, waste reduction programs, and efforts to support local communities. Many hotels are now obtaining green certifications, such as LEED (Leadership in Energy and Environmental Design) or the Global Sustainable Tourism Council's certification, which can guide you in making responsible choices.

One vital aspect of sustainable tourism is plastic reduction. Simple acts like carrying a reusable water bottle or using a cloth shopping bag can significantly decrease plastic waste. Many travel destinations, especially those battling pollution, greatly appreciate tourists who make an effort to reduce single-use plastics. These small but powerful choices contribute to cleaner oceans and healthier terrestrial ecosystems, helping ensure that natural habitats remain vibrant for future visitors.

Cultural preservation is another pillar of sustainable tourism. When visiting new places, it's essential to respect local traditions and lifestyles. Educate yourself on the cultural norms and practices of your destination, and always aim to support local artisans, performers, and guides. Engaging with community-based tourism initiatives allows you to immerse yourself in authentic experiences while also contributing directly to the local economy. This not only enriches your travel experience but also empowers communities to preserve their heritage.

Transportation is a significant factor in sustainable tourism. Air travel, albeit sometimes unavoidable, is one of the largest contributors to carbon emissions in the tourism sector. When possible, consider alternative means of transportation like trains, buses, or boats that have a lower carbon footprint. For shorter distances, cycling or walking offers an even more eco-friendly option, allowing you to explore at a slower pace while reducing environmental impact.

Once you arrive at your destination, personal conduct plays a substantial role. Be mindful of your resource consumption by taking short showers, turning off lights and air conditioning when not in use, and reusing towels and linens. Many eco-friendly hotels are encouraging guests to adopt these habits, and some even offer incentives for eco-conscious behaviors. Demonstrating environmental stewardship during your stay can inspire others to follow suit.

National parks and protected areas are popular destinations for tourists seeking natural beauty and adventure. However, these areas are also incredibly vulnerable to the impacts of high visitor numbers. Stick to marked trails to prevent soil erosion, avoid disturbing wildlife, and adhere to the "Leave No Trace" principles: take only pictures and leave only footprints. Conscientious behavior helps preserve these pristine environments, ensuring they can be enjoyed by future generations.

Wildlife tourism requires special attention. While the prospect of getting up close and personal with exotic animals may be exhilarating, it's essential to choose ethical wildlife tours that don't stress or harm the animals. Avoid attractions that involve petting, feeding, or riding wild animals. Instead, look for operations that prioritize animal welfare and conservation efforts, offering guided tours in natural habitats where animals can be observed behaving as they would in the wild.

Eating locally is another effective way to practice sustainable tourism. Dining at locally owned restaurants and choosing dishes made with regionally sourced ingredients not only supports local economies but also reduces the carbon footprint associated with transporting food. Exploring local markets and trying traditional foods enhances cultural experiences and often leads to delightful culinary discoveries.

Sustainable tourism isn't confined to environmental responsibility alone; social sustainability is equally crucial. Engage with local communities in ways that are respectful and mutually beneficial. Volunteering for local projects, buying from local businesses, and attending community events can all contribute positively. When communities feel the benefits of tourism, they are more likely to invest in conservation and sustainable practices themselves.

One of the most rewarding aspects of sustainable tourism is knowing that your journey contributes to the ongoing health and vibrancy of the world's most beautiful places. When thoughtfully planned and executed, travel can be a powerful force for good. By fostering respectful, mindful, and responsible tourism habits, you're joining a growing movement of travelers who care deeply about the planet and its inhabitants.

A sustainable approach to tourism doesn't mean sacrificing comfort or enjoyment. In fact, many travelers find that eco-friendly practices lead to richer, more memorable experiences. Whether it's through slow travel, which encourages deeper connection to each place, or through eco-adventures that bring you closer to nature, sustainable tourism offers unique opportunities to see the world through a lens of care and responsibility.

As travelers, we hold significant power to shape the future of tourism. By making choices that align with principles of sustainability, we can help protect the world's incredible destinations. The impact of individual efforts may seem small, but collectively, they create a substantial ripple effect across the globe. The next time you plan a trip, let sustainability be your guide—travel lighter, travel mindfully, and travel with purpose. The world awaits, and there's no better way to see it than through the eyes of a responsible tourist.

In conclusion, sustainable tourism practices are an essential part of eco-friendly travel. From planning and transportation to activities and dining, every decision we make as tourists has the potential to contribute positively to the places we visit. By embracing sustainability in our travel habits, we not only enrich our own experiences but also pave the way for future generations to enjoy the same wonders. So, pack your bags with sustainability in mind and embark on your next adventure with a commitment to making a difference.

Low-Impact Travel Destinations

When it comes to eco-friendly travel, the destination you choose plays a significant role in your overall environmental impact. Opting for low-impact travel destinations not only helps minimize your carbon footprint but also supports communities that are committed to sustainable practices. It's a way to blend your love of travel with your love for the planet.

Low-impact travel destinations often feature natural beauty, local culture, and a commitment to conservation. For example, Costa Rica is a country that has made significant strides in sustainable tourism. With over 25% of its landmass protected in national parks and reserves, Costa Rica offers travelers a chance to explore lush rainforests, vibrant wildlife, and pristine beaches all while preserving these natural wonders for future generations.

Another excellent option is Iceland, which is known for its geothermal energy and impressive landscapes. The country uses renewable energy for almost all its electricity and heating needs. Visiting Iceland not only provides awe-inspiring views of glaciers, geysers, and volcanic landscapes but also an education in how countries can harness renewable resources effectively.

On the other side of the world, Bhutan stands as a beacon of sustainable development. The country has adopted a holistic approach to development that focuses on Gross National Happiness rather than Gross Domestic Product. Tourism is tightly regulated; visitors must book travel through certified tour operators, ensuring that tourism remains sustainable and preserves the country's culture and environment.

In North America, the Pacific Northwest offers a wealth of eco-friendly travel opportunities. From Oregon's rugged coastlines to Washington's verdant forests, this region is ripe for exploration. Many cities such as Portland and Seattle have implemented extensive recycling programs, promoted local farm-to-table restaurants, and improved public transit systems, making it easier for visitors to practice sustainable living even while on vacation.

If you're looking for an exotic locale, Madagascar presents a unique opportunity for eco-conscious travelers. This island nation is home to an astonishing array of endemic species, from lemurs to baobab trees. Efforts are ongoing to preserve these unique ecosystems, and eco-lodges and sustainable tour operators are readily available, making it easier for you to contribute positively to conservation efforts while experiencing the island's natural beauty.

Meanwhile, in Australia, Tasmania has become a hub for eco-tourism. Known for its unspoiled wilderness, the island state offers numerous nature reserves and eco-friendly accommodations. From hiking in the Cradle Mountain-Lake St Clair National Park to exploring the Tarkine rainforest, Tasmania provides a host of activities that allow travelers to connect with nature sustainably.

For those who prefer a European adventure, Slovenia offers an excellent mix of green tourism and cultural experiences. The country has invested heavily in sustainable tourism, with many areas promoting nature-based activities such as hiking, cycling, and kayaking. Ljubljana, the capital city, has been awarded the title of European Green Capital, thanks to its car-free zones, extensive green spaces, and commitment to sustainable living.

Venturing to Asia, the island of Bali in Indonesia has become increasingly focused on sustainability. Beyond its beautiful beaches and vibrant culture, Bali is home to numerous eco-friendly resorts, yoga retreats, and organic farms. Many establishments on the island are committed to reducing plastic waste, conserving water, and sourcing local produce, offering travelers a chance to enjoy a luxurious yet responsible holiday.

In Africa, Kenya stands out not only for its incredible wildlife but also for its community-based tourism initiatives. Visiting community conservancies and staying at eco-lodges that focus on wildlife preservation and local empowerment offers a travel experience that's both enriching and environmentally responsible. Walking safaris, bird-watching tours, and staying in tented camps are just some ways to explore Kenya's stunning landscapes without leaving a significant footprint.

The concept of low-impact travel extends beyond just choosing the right destination. It also involves making conscious decisions about how to get there and what to do when you arrive. For example, opting for slower travel methods like trains or boats over flying can significantly reduce your carbon emissions. Once at your destination, prioritize local experiences that support the community, such as eating at local restaurants, purchasing handmade crafts, and participating in community-led tours.

It's also worth mentioning that some of the best low-impact travel experiences can be found close to home. National parks, state parks, and natural reserves offer incredible opportunities to connect with nature without the need for international travel. This not only reduces your carbon footprint but also allows you to explore and appreciate the natural beauty in your own backyard.

Of course, part of the joy of travel is discovering and experiencing new cultures. Low-impact travel destinations often emphasize the importance of cultural exchange and learning. Engaging with local communities, understanding their customs, and participating in traditional activities can enrich your travel experience and foster a deeper connection with the places you visit. It's a way to leave a positive impact rather than just reducing your negative one.

Incorporating sustainable practices while traveling can be easier than you might think. For instance, you can start by choosing eco-friendly accommodations that have received certifications from reputable organizations like Green Key or EarthCheck. These establishments are recognized for their efforts in reducing waste, conserving water, and using renewable energy sources.

Additionally, look for tour operators and travel companies that prioritize sustainability. Many companies now offer eco-friendly packages that include carbon offsetting for flights, accommodations in sustainable hotels, and activities that support local communities and conservation efforts.

Proper packing also plays a role in low-impact travel. Bringing reusable items like water bottles, shopping bags, and utensils can cut down on single-use plastics. Opt for environmentally friendly toiletries and make sure to follow the principles of Leave No Trace to minimize your impact on natural environments.

As you plan your next adventure, it's essential to remember that every choice counts. From the destinations you select to the activities you engage in, each decision can contribute to a more sustainable world. Low-impact travel isn't about sacrificing experiences or luxury; it's about enriching your journey by doing good for the planet and its people.

So, whether you're exploring the rich biodiversity of Costa Rica, the geothermal wonders of Iceland, or the pristine wilderness of Tasmania, low-impact travel offers a fulfilling and sustainable way to see the world. Let's take these steps together towards a future where travel and environmental stewardship go hand in hand, creating memories that don't harm the places we hold dear.

Packing Light and Smart

Packing light isn't just about convenience—it's also a powerful way to lessen your environmental impact when traveling. When you pack less, you're not only reducing the physical burden on your journey but also cutting down on the weight transported by vehicles, which translates to lower fuel consumption and reduced carbon emissions.

Take a moment to ponder your typical packing routine. Are there items you consistently bring but rarely use? Mindful packing means prioritizing only the essentials. Let necessity guide your choices. Opt for multi-functional items that can serve several purposes. For instance, a versatile sarong can work as clothing, a blanket, or even a makeshift bag.

Packing smart also involves selecting eco-friendly products. Instead of dragging along disposable items, consider reusable alternatives. Bring a sturdy water bottle you can refill, which significantly cuts down on plastic waste. A set of travel utensils made of bamboo or stainless steel can replace single-use plastic options.

As you pack, think compactness and efficiency. Organize your belongings to save space and make them easily accessible. Packing cubes can be a game-changer, allowing for partitioned storage within your luggage. They help keep things tidy and make it easier to find what you need without rummaging through your bag.

When it comes to clothing, choose items made from sustainable materials like organic cotton, hemp, or recycled fabrics. These eco-friendly options often require less water and fewer pesticides to produce. Opt for a minimalist wardrobe with versatile pieces that can be mixed and matched. Focus on layers, enabling you to adapt to varying weather conditions without overpacking.

Consider the impacts of your personal care items as well. Travel-sized toiletries might seem practical, but they often result in unnecessary plastic waste. Instead, invest in reusable travel containers that you can fill with your favorite eco-friendly products. Solid shampoos and conditioners, as well as toothpaste tablets, are excellent alternatives to traditional liquid forms. These products often last longer and take up less space.

Electronics are another major category to consider. They are essential but can also be burdensome and resource-intensive. When packing gadgets, bring only what's necessary. Instead of carrying multiple chargers, find one with multiple USB ports. Solar-powered chargers can be an excellent addition, allowing you to harness renewable energy to power your devices.

Thinking about documentation, digital copies can significantly reduce paper waste. Store e-tickets, maps, and reservations on your phone instead of printing them out. If you absolutely need physical copies, try to print double-sided to minimize paper use. Use recycled paper whenever possible.

For longer trips, laundry can weigh heavily on your packing list. Instead of packing numerous outfits, choose less and plan to do laundry on the go. A small, eco-friendly laundry soap can go a long way, and several hotels offer laundry services. Even hand-washing in your accommodation's sink can help you refresh outfits without the need for overpacking.

Your packing approach also extends to the materials you choose for your luggage itself. Sustainable luggage options are made from recycled materials and designed to be durable, thus reducing waste over time. Look for brands committed to sustainability, that offer repair services, ensuring your luggage has a long life and staying out of landfills.

Packing light and smart not only benefits the environment but also enhances your travel experience. It makes moving through airports, bus stations, and hotels more seamless. It leaves you with more energy and less stress, allowing you to focus on the journey and the richness it brings.

To pack light and smart also means being prepared with a mindset open to adapting. Unexpected situations may arise where you need something you didn't pack. Embrace resourcefulness and a community spirit, borrowing or sharing with fellow travelers can reduce the need for everyone to carry duplicate items.

Lastly, remember that packing isn't just a task; it's an opportunity to set the tone for an eco-conscious journey. By being intentional with what you bring, you're making a strong, personal statement about the commitment to living sustainably. It reinforces the idea that every small action contributes to a broader, enduring impact on our planet.

Chapter 11:
Inspirational Stories

While it's easy to feel overwhelmed by the magnitude of environmental challenges, countless individuals and communities have risen to the call of living sustainably, turning aspirations into impactful, tangible actions. Take for instance, Greta Thunberg, a young climate activist whose solo school strike ignited a global movement, reminding us all that one determined voice can spark worldwide change. In regions impacted by climate change, grassroots organizations have assembled to implement renewable energy projects, proving how local initiatives can spearhead broader transformations. Equally compelling are the stories of cities like Copenhagen, which have committed to becoming carbon-neutral by integrating bike-friendly infrastructure and investing in green technologies. Each of these narratives—whether they focus on solitary acts of courage, collective community efforts, or sweeping municipal initiatives—illustrates the boundless potential of dedicated human spirit in fostering a sustainable future. These stories serve as powerful reminders that motivated actions, no matter the scale, weave together the fabric of a greener, healthier planet for generations to come.

Individuals Making a Difference

When talking about environmental change, it's often the monumental achievements of big corporations or sweeping government policies that come to mind. But, real change often begins with individuals and their fervent passion for making the world a better place. Imagine a ripple effect. One small action, driven by a single person, can inspire an entire community to change.

Take the story of Leah Thomas, for example. Leah, an environmentalist and activist, started "Intersectional Environmentalist", a platform that bridges environmental activism with social justice. Her goal was to ensure that marginalized communities have a voice in the environmental conversation. She tirelessly uses her platform to educate and advocate, showing that sustainability isn't just about green energy or recycling, but also about equity and inclusion. Leah's impact? Profound. She's brought an inclusive perspective that's reshaping how we think about environmentalism and who gets to be a part of it.

Similarly, let's reflect on the life of Rob Greenfield. An adventurer and environmentalist, Rob has garnered attention for his radical approach to sustainability. From living off the grid, growing his own food, to producing zero waste for an entire year, Rob's actions are bold demonstrations of what's possible when one truly commits to a sustainable lifestyle. His message is clear: radical change, while daunting, is achievable and often starts with a single brave step toward it.

Then there's the incredible work of Lauren Singer, the founder of "Trash is for Tossers". Frustrated by the immense waste produced by her university, Lauren decided to eliminate disposable plastics from her life. She fit two years' worth of her trash into a mason jar! Her journey into zero waste living wasn't just personal but also deeply public. By documenting her efforts, she inspired thousands to reconsider their own waste habits. Today, her blog and store continue to provide practical advice and products for those looking to minimize their environmental impact.

But it's not only about public figures. Everyday individuals often go unnoticed, yet their contributions are no less significant. Think of the local teacher who's introduced a comprehensive recycling program at her school, engaging and educating young minds on sustainability. Or the community gardener who's transformed an abandoned urban lot into a flourishing green space, offering fresh produce to local families. These unsung heroes might not have vast platforms or global recognition, but their grassroots efforts create tangible, lasting change.

In many cases, the motivation for these individuals is deeply personal. Take Linh Truong, who grew up in a pollution-heavy city. Witnessing the health impacts on her family, Linh became determined to fight for cleaner air and water. She started small by organizing local clean-up drives and advocating for green spaces in urban planning. Over the years, her dedication has blossomed into a full-fledged environmental NGO that works on policy change, public awareness, and sustainable development projects.

Another inspiring individual is Felix Finkbeiner, who started a reforestation initiative called "Plant-for-the-Planet" at the tender age of nine. What began as a school project quickly burgeoned into a global movement, planting millions of trees worldwide. His initiative isn't just about reforestation but education, teaching the next generation the importance of trees in combating climate change. Felix's story shows that age is no barrier when it comes to making a difference. Even the youngest voices can echo loudly and effect meaningful change.

These stories highlight a crucial point: every effort counts. Whether it's through advocacy, lifestyle changes, or community projects, each contribution supports the broader goal of environmental sustainability. The beauty of these individual efforts lies in their relatability. Not everyone can lead a large-scale movement, but anyone can take small steps in their daily life. From reducing personal waste, supporting local and sustainable brands, to advocating for green policies—these actions, though seemingly small, collectively drive significant impact.

Moreover, the success of these individuals reveals the power of storytelling in environmental activism. When people like Leah, Rob, and Lauren share their journeys, they're not just recounting personal achievements—they're crafting narratives that resonate, inspire, and mobilize others. Their stories act as blueprints, showing us that change is possible, practical, and most importantly, necessary.

However, inspiration alone isn't enough. These stories also bring a sense of urgency to our collective consciousness. Climate change, deforestation, and pollution are escalating threats that require immediate action. Individuals making a difference remind us that time is of the essence, and there's much work to be done. They challenge the inertia of complacency and ignite a sense of responsibility in each one of us.

In conclusion, it's individuals making a difference who illuminate the path toward a sustainable future. Their endeavors, whether grand or humble, serve as beacons, guiding us toward actionable and meaningful change. They demonstrate that regardless of our background, resources, or status, everyone has the potential to contribute to environmental conservation. The key takeaway? Don't underestimate the power of one. One idea, one action, one person—it all starts somewhere. Let these stories inspire you to adopt eco-friendly practices in your own life. After all, change begins with you.

Communities Leading the Way

Communities are powerful entities. When individuals unite for a shared cause, their collective effort can lead to extraordinary transformations. Across the globe, communities are taking the lead in sustainable practices, proving that local actions can yield significant environmental benefits. They offer more than just green solutions;

they provide a blueprint for what a collaborative, eco-conscious future can look like.

Take the small town of Kamikatsu in Japan, for example. They've embarked on a zero-waste mission that's nothing short of inspiring. The town has implemented an extensive sorting system where residents separate their trash into 45 distinct categories. It may sound daunting, but it's become second nature to the people of Kamikatsu. Their commitment has led to a remarkable waste reduction, achieving an impressive 80% recycling rate. They demonstrate that meticulous community effort can lead to minor waste.

In another corner of the world, the city of Copenhagen is setting the bar high for urban sustainability. Known for its emphasis on cycling, the city has developed an infrastructure that prioritizes bike lanes over car roads. Approximately 62% of Copenhageners use bicycles for their daily commute. Not only does this reduce carbon emissions, but it fosters a healthier lifestyle. This shift in transportation culture shows how city planning can impact individual behaviors, nudging people towards more sustainable practices.

It's not just about the logistics and infrastructure; it's also about fostering a sense of community. In Detroit, a city synonymous with industrial decline, urban gardening initiatives have blossomed. Vacant lots have been converted into thriving community gardens, providing fresh food and a sense of purpose to local residents. These gardens are not just about growing vegetables; they're about nurturing a community spirit. They offer educational programs for local children and serve as hubs for social activity, creating a ripple effect of positive change.

Innovative waste management systems have also been pioneered in places like San Francisco. Long before it was a fashionable topic, this city pledged to achieve zero waste by 2020. While they didn't entirely hit their target, they made significant strides. Composting has become second nature, and waste diversion rates have soared to around 80%. Their aggressive policies underscore the importance of local government stepping up to lead their citizens towards greener habits.

Communities don't always have to start with large-scale initiatives. Sometimes, the change begins in smaller, more personal settings. In Bristol, England, a "Repair Café" movement is gaining traction. Here, volunteers gather to fix broken household items, from toasters to bicycles, preventing them from ending up in landfills. These cafés are more than just repair shops; they're spaces where people learn valuable skills, share stories, and build relationships. It's a grassroots initiative proving that sustainability can start with simple, restorative actions.

Incorporating green technology has also been a game-changer for some communities. Take the Isle of Eigg, a small island in Scotland, where residents collectively decided to rely on renewable energy sources. Extensive use of wind, solar, and hydroelectric power has made them almost entirely self-sufficient in energy needs. This collective effort reduces their carbon footprint and fosters a sense of independence and resilience.

Still, the road to sustainability isn't without its challenges. Communities often face resistance, whether from cultural inertia or economic constraints. The City of Curitiba in Brazil, famous for its advanced public transit system, had to overcome significant opposition to reduce car dependency. They did so by making the bus system incredibly efficient and affordable, thus turning the tide of public opinion. Their story reminds us that perseverance and innovation can successfully break down even the toughest barriers.

Closer to home, in the United States, Asheville in North Carolina has become a beacon for green building and renewable energy. Community workshops and educational programs have sprung up, teaching residents about sustainable living. Local businesses have joined the effort, adopting eco-friendly practices and driving policy changes that favor renewable energy. The synergy between residents, businesses, and local government has turned Asheville into a model for other cities wishing to go green.

Another remarkable example comes from Germany, where the village of Wildpoldsried has outpaced national efforts toward renewable energy. What's unique about Wildpoldsried is that the residents didn't wait for external mandates; they took action themselves. Wind turbines, solar panels, and biogas facilities now dot the landscape, generating more energy than the village consumes. Their journey has turned into an economic boon, attracting tourism and investments, showing that sustainability can drive financial prosperity too.

But change isn't limited to affluent or technologically advanced communities. Consider the example of the Rwandan village of Gashora. Here, a women's cooperative has spearheaded efforts to combat deforestation by making cleaner cooking stoves. These stoves reduce wood consumption and greenhouse gas emissions. The empowerment of women and the positive environmental impact shows how social and environmental goals can align.

These communities remind us that change happens when people come together with a shared vision and a drive to act. They exemplify the adage that think globally, act locally isn't just a catchy phrase but a potent strategy for real-world transformation. They teach us that we won't make substantial progress unless we involve everyone—young and old, marginalized and privileged. Sustainability must be a collective effort to be effective and equitable.

As we draw inspiration from these stories, it's essential to remember that every community has unique needs and resources. What worked in Kamikatsu or Copenhagen might not be replicateable elsewhere. However, the underlying principle remains the same: when people unite for a cause, their combined action can lead to extraordinary outcomes. The key is to adapt these principles to fit local contexts and challenges.

The overarching lesson from these examples is that a sustainable future is attainable. It's already happening in pockets around the world. These communities provide a roadmap, showing the potential for monumental change through collective action and shared responsibility. They remind us that no step is too small and that every effort counts. Each of us can be a catalyst for change within our communities, turning individual actions into collective wins for the planet.

As you ponder the next steps in your sustainable journey, think about how you might engage your community. Whether starting a local garden, advocating for better public transit, or organizing a repair café, your actions can inspire others to join the movement. After all, it's through these collective efforts that we can hope to create a more sustainable, healthier world for future generations. So, let's take these stories not just as tales of triumph but as blueprints for action. Together, we can lead the way.

Case Studies of Environmental Success

Just as inspiration can be drawn from the actions of individuals and communities, we can also learn much from case studies of environmental success. These cases highlight how effective strategies, commitment, and a dose of ingenuity can transform local landscapes, economies, and communities. Let's explore a few of these remarkable stories where audacious goals met steadfast dedication, resulting in tangible, sustainable outcomes that echo the potential of what's possible.

One impressive example comes from Copenhagen, Denmark, a city that has transformed itself into an icon of urban sustainability. Over the past two decades, Copenhagen has aggressively pursued policies aimed at reducing its carbon footprint, increasing green spaces, and promoting cycling as a primary mode of transportation. The city has invested heavily in infrastructure, creating over 200 miles of cycle lanes, and the results speak volumes. A staggering 62% of Copenhagen's residents commute by bike every day. This not only reduces traffic congestion and air pollution but also promotes a healthier, more active populace.

Moreover, the city's efforts to become carbon-neutral by 2025 have seen significant advancements in renewable energy. Wind turbines pepper the sea just off the coast, providing a substantial portion of the city's energy needs. Public buildings and new developments now incorporate state-of-the-art energy-efficient designs. The collective impact of these measures has made Copenhagen a model city for sustainability, showing that comprehensive planning and community involvement can lead to groundbreaking achievements.

Similarly, the Gaviotas project in Colombia offers an inspiring tale of environmental restoration and socio-economic upliftment. This initiative started in the 1970s when a group of visionaries set out to transform the barren, savanna-like plains of Los Llanos into a thriving, sustainable community. Over the years, the Gaviotas team planted millions of trees, which not only reforested the area but also significantly altered the local microclimate. This reforestation effort brought back rainfall to the region and restored biodiversity, including animals and plants that hadn't been seen in years.

The community didn't stop at just planting trees. They developed low-tech innovations tailored to the needs of rural communities, such as wind-powered water pumps, solar water heaters, and sustainable agriculture practices. These efforts created jobs, improved living conditions, and fostered a culture of innovation and self-reliance. Today, Gaviotas stands as a beacon of what can be achieved through an integrative approach to sustainability, combining environmental restoration with community development.

Australia's Landcare movement is another outstanding example of environmental success driven by grassroots action. Originating in the 1980s, Landcare brings together farmers, land managers, and conservationists to tackle land degradation issues collaboratively. These groups work on various projects, from soil conservation and tree planting to water quality improvement and invasive species control.

The success of Landcare can be attributed to its bottom-up approach, empowering locals to lead initiatives based on their unique knowledge and needs. This has resulted in the restoration of millions of hectares of degraded land, increased biodiversity, and improved agricultural productivity. It also demonstrates how community-led efforts can create synergies between farming and conservation, reversing ecological damage while boosting local economies.

The Isle of Eigg in Scotland provides yet another inspiring case. This small island community decided to break free from dependency on imported fossil fuels by creating its own renewable energy system. In 2008, they launched Eigg Electric, a community-owned company that integrates hydroelectric, wind, and solar power. Today, the island generates virtually all of its electricity through renewable sources, drastically reducing its carbon footprint.

Beyond energy, the community has embraced various sustainable practices, including organic farming, waste reduction, and eco-tourism. These initiatives have revitalized the local economy and attracted a wave of eco-conscious tourists, further proving that sustainability and economic prosperity can go hand in hand. The Isle of Eigg's journey strengthens the case for localized, renewable energy solutions and showcases the power of community-driven change.

Across the Pacific, the city of San Francisco has set the benchmark for urban waste management. San Francisco implemented the goal of sending zero waste to landfills by 2020. By investing in comprehensive recycling and composting programs, supporting legislation that bans non-recyclable plastics, and introducing financial incentives for waste reduction, the city has managed to divert over 80% of its waste from landfills.

San Francisco's strategy hinges not only on innovative waste management systems but also on community education and engagement. Public awareness campaigns and educational programs have played pivotal roles in getting residents and businesses on board with the city's ambitious goals. This approach has inspired other cities worldwide to adopt similar programs, illustrating the global influence that local success stories can wield.

In the business world, Patagonia stands out as a trailblazer in corporate environmental responsibility. This outdoor clothing and gear company has embedded sustainability into its core business strategy. Patagonia's "Worn Wear" program encourages customers to repair and reuse old products, while its stringent supply chain protocols ensure that raw materials are sustainably sourced. The company also actively engages in environmental advocacy, supporting grassroots organizations and initiatives aimed at conserving natural resources.

Patagonia's success demonstrates that businesses can thrive while prioritizing the planet's well-being. By proving that sustainable practices can drive customer loyalty and profitability, Patagonia sets a precedent for other companies to follow. They show that small, focused actions combined with unwavering principles can lead to substantial environmental and economic returns.

India's Barefoot College presents another instance of innovative environmental action. This initiative empowers rural women by training them to become solar engineers. These women, often grandmothers, learn to install, repair, and maintain solar lighting systems in their villages. This has not only improved the quality of life in these communities by providing reliable, clean energy but also elevated the status and skills of women, often considered the backbone of rural societies.

Barefoot College underscores the transformative power of sustainable solutions tailored to the unique needs of communities. By focusing on education and local empowerment, they've created a model that can be adapted to various contexts globally, spreading the seeds of sustainable development far and wide.

These case studies collectively emphasize the enormous potential for change when communities and organizations commit to sustainable practices. Whether it's through innovative urban planning, local environmental stewardship, renewable energy initiatives, or corporate responsibility, the examples set by these pioneers illuminate pathways to a more sustainable future. They remind us that significant impact often starts with small, decisive actions and that every individual and community has the potential to contribute to global environmental well-being.

In harnessing these models of success, we can build on their lessons, replicate their strategies, and ultimately craft our own stories of environmental achievement. By drawing inspiration from these diverse examples, each of us can find ways to integrate sustainability into our daily lives, fostering a world where ecology and economy harmoniously coexist.

Chapter 12:
The Future of Sustainability

The dawn of burgeoning technologies and progressive policies presents a beacon of hope for the future of sustainability. As we stand at the threshold of unprecedented advancements ranging from renewable energy innovations to smart urban planning, our collective actions today shape the destinies of generations to come. Governments worldwide are increasingly enacting robust legislation aimed at curbing environmental degradation, promoting green jobs, and incentivizing eco-friendly practices. Yet, the power to drive meaningful change rests not only in lawmakers' hands but also in our daily choices—embracing circular economies, advocating for systemic change, and fostering a culture of sustainability in our communities. The road ahead is challenging, but with determination and a shared vision, we can transform our world into a resilient, thriving haven where ecological balance prospers. Let's plant the seeds now for a flourishing, sustainable tomorrow.

Emerging Green Technologies

In a world where climate change and environmental degradation are pressing issues, emerging green technologies shine like beacons of hope, illuminating the path toward a more sustainable future. These trailblazing innovations are not just concepts for tech enthusiasts; they hold the potential to revolutionize the way we live, produce, and consume, making eco-friendly lifestyles more achievable than ever.

Some of these technologies focus on harnessing renewable energy sources, aiming to reduce our dependency on fossil fuels. Solar power, for instance, has made considerable strides with advancements like thin-film solar cells and bifacial modules, which offer greater efficiency and versatility. While rooftop solar panels are becoming a fixture in many neighborhoods, community solar projects are also gaining traction. These initiatives allow multiple households to benefit from a shared solar array, democratizing access to cleaner energy and reducing utility costs across the board.

Wind energy has evolved too, with innovations like vertical-axis wind turbines and airborne wind energy systems. These technologies promise higher efficiency and reduced environmental impact compared to traditional wind turbines. Offshore wind farms, located out at sea, harness stronger and more consistent wind currents, providing a robust and reliable source of renewable energy. By tapping into these advances, communities can drive towards a future where clean energy powers homes, schools, and businesses without the detrimental effects of carbon emissions.

Energy storage solutions play an equally crucial role in maximizing the utility of renewable energy. Battery technologies such as lithium-ion and next-generation solid-state batteries are continually improving, making it possible to store excess energy produced during peak production times effectively. Home battery systems integrated with solar panels allow households to maintain a reliable energy supply even when the sun isn't shining. Larger-scale storage solutions, like grid batteries, provide similar benefits to entire communities, ensuring a stable and resilient power infrastructure.

In the realm of transportation, electric vehicles (EVs) are no longer a distant dream but a burgeoning reality. The latest models offer longer driving ranges, faster charging times, and lower maintenance costs, making them a viable alternative to traditional gas-powered vehicles.

Innovations in battery technology, particularly the development of solid-state batteries, promise to further extend driving ranges and reduce charging times, making EVs even more attractive. Moreover, advancements in charging infrastructure, such as ultra-fast charging stations and wireless charging technology, are making it easier and more convenient for drivers to make the switch.

Public transportation systems are also undergoing significant green transformations. Electric buses and trains, powered by renewable energy sources, are now operational in numerous cities worldwide. Additionally, smart transportation systems integrating artificial intelligence (AI) and the Internet of Things (IoT) can optimize routes and reduce congestion, leading to decreased emissions and energy consumption. Even traditional forms of transport are getting eco-friendly upgrades, with biofuels and hydrogen fuel cells offering cleaner alternatives to gasoline and diesel.

Emerging green technologies are making substantial leaps in the sphere of building and construction as well. Innovations like biophilic design and green roofs are not only aesthetically pleasing but also reduce energy consumption and improve air quality. Materials science is giving us stronger, lighter, and more sustainable building materials like mass timber, carbon-sequestering concrete, and recycled steel. These materials reduce the carbon footprint of construction projects and contribute to a healthier living environment. Imagine a city skyline where every building is a self-sustaining ecosystem, teeming with greenery and life, nurturing both its inhabitants and the environment.

Smart home technologies allow homeowners to monitor and optimize their energy consumption like never before. Smart thermostats, lighting systems, and energy-efficient appliances can be controlled remotely via smartphones or automated based on usage patterns, enhancing convenience while reducing energy waste. Combined with renewable energy sources and home battery systems, these technologies can transform traditional homes into net-zero energy homes, where the energy consumed is equal to the energy produced.

Water conservation technology is another critical frontier with groundbreaking solutions coming to the fore. Innovations such as atmospheric water generators can extract water directly from the air, providing a sustainable water source even in arid regions. Advanced irrigation systems, using AI and IoT, ensure that water is used efficiently in agriculture, reducing waste and promoting better crop yields. Greywater recycling systems enable households to reuse water from sinks, showers, and washing machines for non-potable purposes like irrigation and toilet flushing, significantly cutting down on freshwater usage.

In the world of manufacturing, green technologies are making waves with sustainable practices and materials. Additive manufacturing, or 3D printing, minimizes waste by using only the exact amount of material needed for each product. Innovations in bioplastics, made from renewable biomass sources, offer a biodegradable alternative to petroleum-based plastics, reducing the environmental impact of plastic waste. Similarly, advancements in recycling technologies are enabling the recovery and reuse of materials from electronic waste, textiles, and even construction debris, promoting a circular economy where resources are continuously reused rather than discarded.

The agricultural sector, too, is seeing a surge of green innovation. Precision farming, powered by drones, satellites, and sensor technology, allows farmers to monitor crop conditions in real-time, optimizing water, fertilizer, and pesticide use. Vertical farming and hydroponics, which grow plants in vertically stacked layers or nutrient-rich water, respectively, maximize space and resource efficiency, enabling fresh produce to be grown closer to urban centers and reducing the carbon footprint of food transportation.

Of course, the implementation of these technologies isn't without challenges. Cost, scalability, and public acceptance can all pose significant barriers. However, as these technologies continue to develop and gain traction, we can expect economies of scale to drive down costs and make green innovations more accessible to the general public. Much like the rise of the internet or smartphones, what once seemed futuristic can quickly become an integral part of everyday life.

What about the role of policy in accelerating these advancements? Governments and institutions have a vital part to play by providing incentives for research, development, and adoption of green technologies. Legislative measures like subsidies, tax incentives, and regulatory frameworks can help create a more favorable environment for these innovations to thrive. Additionally, public awareness campaigns can educate and inspire individuals to support and adopt green technologies, fostering a culture of sustainability.

Our journey towards sustainability is undeniably complex, yet the advent of these emerging green technologies offers a compelling hope. They are the catalysts driving us closer to a world where our demand for resources doesn't compromise the planet's ability to regenerate. By actively engaging with these technologies and supporting their adoption, we can each play our part in fostering a sustainable, resilient, and harmonious future.

Incorporating emerging green technologies into your life means more than just reducing your environmental footprint—it signifies a commitment to live in harmony with the Earth. Whether you choose to install solar panels, switch to an electric vehicle, or incorporate smart home technologies, remember, each step, no matter how small, is a stride toward a sustainable future. The key lies in embracing these innovations with an open mind and a willing heart. Only then can we unlock the full potential of a greener tomorrow.

Policy and Legislation

When we consider the future of sustainability, we mustn't overlook the pivotal role that policy and legislation play. Governments and regulatory bodies have the power to set the stage for widespread environmental change. The laws and policies enacted by local, state, and national governments create the framework within which individuals and businesses operate, making them crucial levers for driving sustainability efforts on a grand scale.

Historically, policy and legislation have catalyzed some of the most significant environmental improvements. Take, for instance, the Clean Air Act in the United States, which has led to dramatic reductions in air pollution. But these advancements did not come without a fight. Legislative battles were intense, requiring a collective push from activists, community leaders, and environmentally-conscious citizens.

One of the main challenges is the often slow and cumbersome process of policy-making. It requires extensive research, stakeholder consultations, and, sometimes, tough compromises. Yet, when effective policies are finally enacted, their impact can be profound and long-lasting.

Moving forward, recent policies targeting renewable energy adoption offer enormous potential. Incentives for solar and wind energy have not only boosted renewable energy use but have also made clean energy sources more affordable for average households. Countries like Germany and Denmark have led the way with aggressive renewable energy policies, serving as a model for what's possible.

But policy doesn't stop at energy. Building standards and regulations also play a crucial role. Requiring new constructions to meet high-efficiency standards or incorporating green building materials can significantly cut down on energy use and waste. For example, California's stringent building codes have made it a leader in sustainable housing, setting benchmarks for other states to follow.

In Europe, the push for a circular economy is gaining momentum. Policies aimed at reducing waste and promoting recycling and reuse could revolutionize how products are designed and consumed. By encouraging product designs that prioritize durability, reparability, and recyclability, such legislation aims to keep materials in use for as long as possible.

Policy can also drive change in transportation. Initiatives like California's Zero Emission Vehicle (ZEV) mandate require automakers to produce a certain percentage of electric vehicles (EVs). This not only accelerates the transition to greener transportation options but also prompts innovation within the auto industry. Public transportation systems also benefit from policy support, as government funding can improve the efficiency and reach of transit networks.

Water conservation policies are another crucial area. By setting limits on water usage and encouraging the adoption of water-efficient technologies, governments can significantly reduce water waste. Some regions have implemented water pricing structures that encourage conservation by making excessive water use more costly.

Yet, ambitious policies often face opposition. Lobbying efforts by industries that benefit from the status quo can pose significant hurdles. It's essential for environmentally-conscious individuals to remain vigilant and actively support policies that drive sustainability. Grassroots movements and public opinion can exert powerful pressure on lawmakers to act in favor of environmental interests.

Further, international agreements like the Paris Agreement demonstrate the power of collective action. By setting global targets for reducing greenhouse gas emissions, such treaties create a unified vision for sustainability that crosses national borders. However, the success of these agreements depends on individual countries implementing and adhering to their commitments.

Local governments are not to be overlooked, either. City-level policies can drive substantial change, offering a more immediate and direct impact on residents' daily lives. Urban areas are increasingly adopting "green cities" initiatives, focusing on everything from public transportation improvements to green spaces and waste management systems.

Digital policy tools can also play an influential role in promoting sustainability. Online platforms and apps designed to help people track their carbon footprints or find sustainable products can be significantly boosted through supportive regulations and incentives.

Looking ahead, as new technologies and innovations emerge, policies must adapt swiftly to incorporate and promote these advancements. Innovations in renewable energy, like advanced battery storage or small-scale wind turbines, need policy frameworks that encourage their adoption and integration into existing systems.

In summary, policy and legislation serve as the bedrock for the future of sustainability. While the path to enacting these policies may be fraught with challenges, the potential benefits make the journey worthwhile. From renewable energy and building standards to water conservation and transportation, effective legislation can create a more sustainable world for future generations. Our collective voices and actions can ensure that the right policies are put in place and that they drive meaningful environmental change.

As we move forward, remember that policy is not a distant, abstract concept. It's a tool within our reach, one that can profoundly shape the world. By staying informed, advocating for change, and holding policymakers accountable, we can help forge a sustainable future rooted in strong, effective legislation.

How You Can Shape the Future

In the grand tapestry of life, each thread—the decisions we make daily—counts. If you're wondering how you can make a tangible impact on our planet's future, know that you hold more power than you might imagine. Every small action creates ripples that expand outward, influence others, and ultimately contribute to a more sustainable world. This section will outline practical steps you can implement in your life today, guiding you toward becoming an active participant in the sustainable movement.

Changing the path of our planet starts with changing ourselves. The first step is to cultivate a mindset that prioritizes sustainability in every aspect of life. Whether it's through simple daily habits or larger lifestyle shifts, your commitment to eco-friendly living serves as a beacon, encouraging those around you to follow suit. Think of it as a domino effect; one person's action can inspire a community.

Let's begin with examining your daily routines. From the moment you wake up, there are opportunities to make more sustainable choices. Switching from disposable to reusable products, such as metal straws, bamboo toothbrushes, and cloth napkins, can reduce waste significantly. Every decision to refuse a plastic bag or single-use cup is a victory, however small it may seem.

Energy Conservation: Have you ever considered just how much energy you consume without realizing it? Turn off lights when they're not in use, unplug devices, and consider switching to energy-efficient appliances. Even adjusting your thermostat by a couple of degrees can lead to noticeable energy savings. A mindful approach to your energy use can make a huge difference.

Water conservation is another vital aspect of shaping a sustainable future. Installing water-saving fixtures, like low-flow showerheads and faucets, can significantly reduce your water usage. You might also take shorter showers and only run dishwashers or laundry machines when they are fully loaded. These actions don't just save water—they help reduce the energy required to heat and pump that water.

While personal actions are critical, building a sustainable future also involves community engagement. Volunteering for or starting local environmental initiatives can amplify your impact. Participate in community clean-up events, tree-planting drives, or workshops on sustainability. These activities not only contribute practically but also foster a sense of collective responsibility and purpose.

Educating others is an equally powerful tool. Share your knowledge and experiences with friends, family, and coworkers. The more people understand the importance and ease of living sustainably, the more likely they are to adopt similar practices. Tools like social media can be invaluable for spreading awareness and rallying collective action.

Eating sustainably is another crucial part of the puzzle. Opt for locally grown, organic foods to reduce the carbon footprint associated with transporting goods. Reducing meat consumption, even slightly, can have a significant environmental impact. If space allows, try your hand at home gardening. Growing your own herbs or vegetables can be exceptionally rewarding—both for you and the planet.

Mindful Consumption: When purchasing items, ask yourself if you truly need them and if they are sustainably produced. Prioritize products with minimal packaging, and opt for second-hand or upcycled options whenever possible. Your choices can guide businesses toward more sustainable practices.

Delving deeper into your consumer habits, reconsider your fashion choices. Fast fashion contributes enormously to environmental degradation. Commit to buying less and choosing quality over quantity. Sustainable brands, thrift stores, and clothing swaps offer eco-friendly alternatives.

Transportation choices also play a significant role. Whenever possible, opt for walking, biking, or public transit over driving. If you need to drive, consider carpooling or using electric or hybrid vehicles. You'll not only reduce your carbon emissions but also promote healthier living environments.

As we navigate this journey, it's vital to remain informed and adaptive. Emerging green technologies are constantly evolving, offering new ways to enhance sustainability. Support policy and legislation that aim to protect our environment. Voting for leaders who prioritize sustainability and advocating for environmental regulations can lead to systemic change.

The influence you wield extends beyond your immediate actions. By supporting businesses that prioritize sustainability and holding accountable those that don't, you help steer the market toward eco-friendly practices. This collective economic pressure can drive large-scale environmental improvements.

One often overlooked but immensely impactful action is investing in renewable energy, whether on a household scale with solar panels or through green energy plans available from many utilities. These choices significantly alter our energy landscape, moving us closer to a reliance on clean, sustainable sources.

Consider the importance of lifelong learning in this domain. Stay Curious about sustainability topics, attend workshops, subscribe to eco-friendly blogs, and read books on environmental issues. The more knowledgeable you are, the more effectively you can act and inspire others.

An essential part of shaping the future is also about redefining success. Success shouldn't be measured solely by financial wealth but by the health of our planet and communities. Fostering a connection with nature, appreciating the simple, sustainable joys of life, and prioritizing well-being over consumption can lead to a more fulfilling life.

Preservation and Advocacy: Gets involved in preserving local ecosystems and advocating for environmental protection. Support conservation projects that safeguard wildlife and natural habitats.

Lastly, remember that progress, not perfection, is the goal. It's easy to feel overwhelmed or disheartened by the immensity of global environmental challenges. But even the smallest steps are steps forward. Celebrate your victories and learn from setbacks, always pushing towards a more sustainable world.

The future of sustainability rests in the collective power of individuals committed to making a difference. By embedding eco-friendly choices into the fabric of daily life, engaging with and inspiring our communities, and supporting systemic changes, we can play an instrumental role in crafting a greener, healthier future for generations to come. Indeed, the power is in your hands.

Conclusion

As we've traversed the myriad paths toward a sustainable lifestyle together, it's vital to recognize that every small step contributes to a larger movement. This book aimed to arm you with knowledge, strategies, and inspiration to embark on or deepen your journey toward eco-friendly living. By now, you should have an extensive toolkit filled with practical advice that can be easily applied in everyday life. But, the journey doesn't end here—it's only just beginning.

Living sustainably is more than adopting practices; it's a mindset shift. Imagine a world where our efforts to reduce waste, minimize our carbon footprint, and make ethical consumer choices are second nature. Picture your communities rallying around green initiatives, creating a ripple effect that transcends city and country borders. Your small actions, when combined with those of others, can lead to profound environmental change.

Let's take a moment to reflect on the importance of historical perspectives. Understanding how our consumption and conservation patterns evolved provides critical insights. We have the knowledge and capacity to avoid the mistakes of the past and innovate for a better future. History teaches us resilience and adaptability, showing that sustainable living is not merely a trend but a return to responsible stewardship.

Reducing waste doesn't have to be a daunting task. Simple practices like composting and creating DIY cleaning products can significantly cut down household waste. These actions make a tangible difference and empower you to reclaim control over the waste you generate. Embrace the 3 R's wholeheartedly—reduce, reuse, recycle— not as a checklist but as guiding principles in your daily life.

Minimizing your carbon footprint may seem complex initially, but it becomes manageable with targeted efforts. By implementing energy-efficient measures in your home and opting for renewable energy sources, you reduce your environmental impact and enjoy cost savings over time. Consider the broader ecological benefits and personal satisfaction derived from making your home as energy-efficient as possible.

Transportation is another key area where you can make substantial changes. Shifting to public transit or cycling over driving can significantly reduce emissions. Embracing electric or hybrid vehicles further underscores your commitment to sustainability. Each time you choose an eco-friendly mode of transport, you set an example and contribute to a cleaner, healthier planet.

Food choices are pivotal in your journey toward sustainable living. Supporting local and organic farmers not only ensures better nutrition but also reduces your carbon footprint. Home gardening, even on a small scale, promotes a deeper connection to the food you consume. By making these conscious choices, you challenge unsustainable agricultural practices and champion sustainable food systems.

Water conservation requires similar considerations. Efficient water use and methods like rainwater harvesting can have a profound impact. Switching to native plants and xeriscaping not only conserves water but enhances local biodiversity. When you prioritize water conservation, you contribute to the sustainability of this finite resource, ensuring it remains available for future generations.

Green home improvements, from eco-friendly materials to smart home technologies, offer tangible benefits. These upgrades not only make your living spaces healthier but also reduce your environmental footprint. Sustainable interior design choices look beyond aesthetics, incorporating elements that reflect your values and commitment to the planet.

Ethical consumerism is about making informed choices, recognizing the impact that each purchase has on the environment and society. Choosing sustainable brands and avoiding fast fashion are acts of resistance against unsustainable industries. Embrace mindful shopping habits, prioritizing quality and sustainability over quantity and trendiness.

Community involvement is crucial. By participating in local environmental initiatives and volunteer opportunities, you build a support network of like-minded individuals. Together, you amplify your impact and contribute to a collective momentum toward sustainability. Your community can serve as a model, inspiring others and fostering a culture of environmental responsibility.

Sustainable travel practices highlight the importance of conscientious living even when you're away from home. Opt for low-impact destinations and pack thoughtfully to reduce your travel footprint. Embrace the journey with a spirit of exploration, mindful of your impact on the places you visit and the cultures you encounter.

The inspirational stories shared in this book underscore the profound impact individuals and communities can have. These narratives serve as powerful reminders that change is possible and that each of us has a role to play. Draw strength and motivation from these examples, knowing that your efforts contribute to a global tapestry of environmental stewardship.

Looking to the future, emerging green technologies and supportive policy frameworks present new opportunities. Stay informed and engaged, advocating for policies that prioritize sustainability. Your voice matters and can influence decisions at all levels. By shaping the future, you help build a world where environmental sustainability is woven into the fabric of daily life.

To sustain this momentum, continually educate yourself and others. Use the resources provided in the appendix to deepen your understanding and expand your network of support. Expect challenges, but know that each one is an opportunity for growth and innovation. Embrace this journey with an open heart and resilient spirit.

With every decision, every action, you're not just reducing your footprint—you're leaving a green legacy. A world in which future generations can thrive, a world that celebrates and respects the natural balance of our ecosystems. Your journey toward sustainability is a meaningful and impactful one. Let it inspire others, and remember, the power to make a change rests in your hands.

Now is the time to act. Let's make our planet a place where harmony with nature prevails over exploitation. Let's build a sustainable, beautiful world—together.

Appendix A:
Appendix

As we reach the final pages of this book, we've laid out numerous paths toward a more sustainable lifestyle. Whether you've been drawn to reducing your waste, minimizing your carbon footprint, or diving into ethical consumerism, there's no shortage of ways to make a positive impact. In this appendix, you'll find additional tools and resources to deepen your understanding and continue your journey toward a greener future.

Resources for Further Reading

Knowledge is power, and staying informed can provide the motivation to keep pushing forward. Here are some recommended books, articles, and websites to expand your learning:

"The Sixth Extinction: An Unnatural History" by Elizabeth Kolbert – A profound look at biodiversity loss and its impacts.

"No Impact Man" by Colin Beavan – A firsthand account of one man's attempt to live a zero-impact life.

"Drawdown: The Most Comprehensive Plan Ever Proposed to Reverse Global Warming" edited by Paul Hawken – A groundbreaking collection of solutions to address climate change.

Website: Earth911 – Offers a plethora of recycling tips and eco-friendly hacks.

Website: Treehugger – An all-encompassing resource on green living and sustainability.

Sustainable Product Guides

Transitioning to eco-friendly products can sometimes feel overwhelming. To help, we've compiled a list of guides that can steer you in the right direction:

Reusable Household Items: Look for guides on alternatives to single-use plastics, such as silicone sandwich bags, beeswax wraps, and stainless steel straws.

Eco-friendly Cleaning Products: Seek out brands that use natural ingredients and sustainable packaging. Guides often highlight popular options like vinegar, baking soda, and essential oil-based cleaners.

Green Energy Solutions: From solar panels to wind turbines, a good guide on renewable energy products can make the transition smoother for your home.

Sustainable Fashion: Check guides that focus on materials like organic cotton, bamboo, and recycled fabrics, which help reduce your wardrobe's environmental footprint.

Contact Information for Environmental Organizations

Getting involved with organizations dedicated to environmental conservation can amplify your impact. Here are a few key groups to consider:

Environmental Defense Fund (EDF): www.edf.org

World Wildlife Fund (WWF): www.worldwildlife.org

Greenpeace: www.greenpeace.org

Natural Resources Defense Council (NRDC): www.nrdc.org

This appendix aims to be a helpful resource as you continue your sustainable living journey. The information provided here is just a starting point; the true change lies in how you apply what you've learned and inspire others to join you. Remember, every small step counts, and together, we can make a significant impact.

Resources for Further Reading

Venturing further into the realm of sustainable living requires a commitment to constant learning and awareness. The journey doesn't end with this book; it's merely the beginning. Here are some resources that offer invaluable insights into sustainable practices, enabling you to dig deeper and find new ways to make a positive environmental impact.

First and foremost, consider diving into comprehensive websites like the *Environmental Protection Agency (EPA)* or *Green America*. These platforms provide extensive information on various topics from reducing waste to energy conservation, along with a plethora of practical guides and tips.

Books are another fantastic way to continue your education. Works such as "Silent Spring" by Rachel Carson and "Cradle to Cradle" by William McDonough & Michael Braungart have become seminal texts in environmental literature. Their insightful investigations into the impacts of human activity on nature can truly transform your perspective.

For those who prefer ongoing updates and community interaction, blogs and online forums can be excellent resources. Websites like *TreeHugger* and *Grist* offer articles, updates, and community advice on living sustainably. These platforms not only provide knowledge but also foster a sense of community among like-minded individuals striving to make a difference.

If you're interested in podcasts, look no further than "The Sustainable Minimalists" or "The Zero Waste Countdown." These podcasts break down complex sustainability topics into understandable bites, making them perfect for listening during your morning commute or while relaxing at home.

Moreover, for the visual learners among you, documentaries can offer profound insights. Films such as "The True Cost," which examines the fashion industry's toll on the environment, and "Before the Flood," which explores global climate change, serve as both educational tools and calls to action.

University research centers and institutes are also treasure troves of information. Institutions like the *Yale School of the Environment* and the *Centre for Alternative Technology* publish papers, reports, and case studies that can offer more scientific depth to your understanding of sustainability.

For those inclined towards activism and community involvement, local environmental organizations and initiatives provide ample opportunities to get involved. Websites like *VolunteerMatch* can help you find volunteering opportunities that align with your skills and interests.

Lastly, don't overlook the power of social media. Accounts dedicated to environmental conservation, such as those run by influencers in the sustainability space, offer daily inspiration and tips on how to integrate eco-friendly habits into your routine.

Arming yourself with knowledge from these diverse sources enables you to make informed choices and take meaningful actions. Sustainability is not a destination but a continuous path of learning and improving. The more you know, the more empowered you become to make impactful changes.

Sustainable Product Guides

Embarking on a sustainable lifestyle isn't just about changing habits but also about making informed choices when it comes to the products we use daily. Sustainable products offer a way to lessen our environmental impact, support ethical practices, and often provide superior quality. In this section, we'll explore guides for selecting and using sustainable products that can seamlessly integrate into your life and elevate your contribution to environmental conservation.

First and foremost, understanding what constitutes a sustainable product is essential. Generally, sustainable products have minimal negative impacts on the environment and society during their lifecycle—production, use, and disposal. They often emphasize biodegradability, ethical labor practices, and minimal carbon footprint in their manufacturing processes. When evaluating products, look for recognized certifications like Fair Trade, USDA Organic, and Energy Star. These labels act as beacons, ensuring that the products you purchase align with sustainable and ethical standards.

Let's dive into sustainable alternatives in different categories of our day-to-day lives:

Sustainable Personal Care Products

Our daily routines often start and end with personal care products. Unfortunately, many conventional options are laden with chemicals and come in non-recyclable packaging. Pivot to sustainable brands that use natural, organic ingredients and eco-friendly packaging. For instance, swap out your plastic toothbrush for one made of bamboo.

Consider using shampoo and conditioner bars instead of bottled versions. They're not only effective but also reduce plastic waste. Deodorants and toothpaste can also be found in plastic-free alternatives, often packaged in glass jars or recyclable metal tins. Supporting brands that prioritize transparency in their ingredient lists and labor practices helps push the market toward healthier, more sustainable standards.

Sustainable Kitchen and Dining

The kitchen, being the heart of many homes, offers numerous opportunities for sustainable practices. Start by swapping single-use disposables with reusable and durable alternatives. Cloth napkins, stainless steel straws, and beeswax wraps are some simple swaps that can significantly cut down waste.

When it comes to cookware and utensils, invest in high-quality, long-lasting items like cast iron pans and wooden spoons. Not only do they reduce the frequency of replacement, but they also bring a certain charm and durability to your kitchen. For food storage, consider glass containers or stainless steel bento boxes over plastic variants. These choices are not only more eco-friendly but can keep your food fresher for longer.

Additionally, choose dish soaps and detergents that come in compostable packaging or aim to refill your existing containers from bulk stores. It's small changes like these that collectively make a big difference.

Clothing and Accessories

The fashion industry is notorious for its environmental impact, from water usage to pollution. However, by making mindful choices, you can reduce your fashion footprint. Look for clothing brands that use organic cotton, bamboo, or recycled materials. These fabrics not only require less water and pesticides during production but are also often biodegradable.

Before making new purchases, consider the possibilities of second-hand shopping. Thrift stores offer unique finds that are kinder to the planet and your wallet. If new clothes are necessary, prioritize brands that adhere to fair trade practices and environmental stewardship.

Eco-friendly accessories, such as bags made from recycled materials or jewelry crafted from sustainable sources, also contribute to lowering your environmental impact. Every purchase is a vote for the kind of world you want to live in.

Home Cleaning Products

Our quest for cleanliness shouldn't come at the environment's expense. Conventional cleaning products often contain harmful chemicals that can pollute waterways and harm aquatic life. Instead, opt for eco-friendly alternatives, which are equally effective but much safer for the planet.

Products boasting labels like 'biodegradable' and 'non-toxic' are significant markers of eco-friendliness. Additionally, many natural products like vinegar, baking soda, and essential oils can be used to make effective DIY cleaning solutions at a fraction of the environmental cost. Package-free or bulk buying options can reduce your plastic footprint while keeping your home spotless.

Technology and Electronics

Although electronics are indispensable in today's world, their environmental toll is staggering. To tread lightly, consider electronics from companies that prioritize sustainability through energy-efficient designs, recyclable materials, and ethical labor practices. Refurbished or second-hand electronics are also excellent choices, extending the life of gadgets that might otherwise end up in landfills.

Energy-efficient appliances, marked by Energy Star ratings, can significantly reduce your energy consumption and utility bills, all the while conserving valuable resources. When disposing of old electronics, always seek proper e-waste recycling programs to ensure they are handled responsibly.

Eco-Friendly Furniture and Home Decor

Furniture and home decor choices also play a significant role in sustainability. Materials like reclaimed wood, bamboo, and recycled metal are excellent choices for reducing environmental impact. Additionally, seek out companies that produce furniture with minimal VOCs (volatile organic compounds) to ensure safer indoor air quality.

Vintage and second-hand furniture can bring a unique charm to your home while circumventing the need for new resources. Whenever possible, support artisans and local craftsmen who create stunning, sustainable pieces that can serve as both functional items and conversation starters.

Sustainable Office Supplies

Our workspaces can be green too. Look for office supplies made from recycled materials, such as paper, pens, and folders. Energy-efficient lighting and the use of natural light can also create a more sustainable office environment.

Reducing paper usage through digital note-taking tools, reusing printer paper, and integrating a comprehensive recycling program can all make a big difference. Additionally, choosing office furniture made from sustainable resources ensures that your workspace reflects your commitment to sustainability.

Gardening and Outdoor Products

Gardening offers a plethora of opportunities to embrace sustainability. Choose organic fertilizers, mulch, and pest control options to keep your garden thriving while being kind to the environment. For tools and equipment, opt for items made from sustainable materials like bamboo or recycled plastics.

Rain barrels for water collection and compost bins for organic waste recycling are fantastic additions to any eco-friendly garden. These choices not only reduce your environmental impact but also enhance the health and productivity of your green spaces.

By making these conscious choices in various aspects of your life, you weave sustainability into the fabric of daily living. The products you choose are powerful instruments, not just in reducing your ecological footprint but as declarations of your values.

Remember, the journey toward a sustainable lifestyle is a continuum of choices, each one building on the previous. By opting for products that champion sustainability and ethical practices, you are not only contributing to a healthier planet but also inspiring those around you to consider their own choices.

Contact Information for Environmental Organizations

Connecting with environmental organizations is instrumental in propelling your efforts toward living a more sustainable lifestyle. These organizations often offer resources, volunteer opportunities, workshops, and advocacy networks that can amplify your contribution to environmental preservation.

Let's explore some critical groups that cater to a variety of environmental causes. Each one has a unique focus, from combating climate change to conserving biodiversity. By reaching out to these organizations, you can find specific ways to get involved that resonate with your personal values and interests.

Greenpeace: Known globally for its activism and campaigns to protect the environment, Greenpeace frequently works on issues such as deforestation, melting ice caps, and plastic pollution. Visit their website to learn more about volunteer opportunities and to join their campaigns.
Website: www.greenpeace.org
Email: info@greenpeace.org

World Wildlife Fund (WWF): If you're passionate about wildlife conservation, the WWF focuses on protecting endangered species and their habitats. They offer programs that allow you to adopt animals, support conservation efforts, and participate in global initiatives.
Website: www.worldwildlife.org
Email: contact@wwfus.org

The Sierra Club: One of the oldest environmental organizations, the Sierra Club engages in multiple facets of environmental advocacy, including conservation, renewable energy promotion, and reducing environmental toxins. Their local chapters provide numerous ways to get involved.
Website: www.sierraclub.org
Email: information@sierraclub.org

Natural Resources Defense Council (NRDC): The NRDC leverages law and science to protect our planet. They tackle issues from climate change to toxic chemicals and have a wealth of resources aimed at empowering individuals to take action.
Website: www.nrdc.org
Email: nrdcinfo@nrdc.org

Environment America: Focusing on environmental advocacy at both the federal and state levels, Environment America works on numerous campaigns related to clean energy, preserving public lands, and clean water initiatives. They often have actionable tools and guides for making your voice heard by policymakers.

Website: www.environmentamerica.org
Email: info@environmentamerica.org

When seeking involvement, it's beneficial to start by visiting the websites of these organizations. Many offer newsletters, action alerts, and social media groups where you can stay informed about current campaigns and events. Subscribing to these can keep you updated and motivated.

Moreover, don't underestimate the impact of smaller, local environmental organizations. These groups often address issues most directly related to your community and can offer more tangible ways to contribute. A simple internet search for "environmental organizations near me" can yield fruitful results.

In addition to larger organizations, many grass-roots movements are driving change at the community level. These movements can be just as impactful and often provide more personalized and immediate ways for you to get involved. They frequently need volunteers, whether it's participating in a local clean-up effort, joining a community garden, or advocating for policy changes at town meetings.

Here's a short list to consider looking into:

Local Audubon Societies: Focused on bird conservation, local Audubon societies offer bird-watching events, habitat restoration projects, and educational workshops. Check the National Audubon Society website to find a chapter near you.

Surfrider Foundation: This global organization is dedicated to protecting the world's oceans, waves, and beaches through a network of grassroots activists. Local chapters often organize beach cleanups and educational events.

Friends of the Earth: An international network, Friends of the Earth focuses on environmental justice and sustainability. They work on issues ranging from climate change to biodiversity, and you can get involved through local campaigns and initiatives.

350.org: Focused primarily on climate change, 350.org is known for its global, grassroots climate movement. They organize events and campaigns aimed at reducing carbon dioxide levels and increasing renewable energy adoption.

Environmental Working Group (EWG): EWG specializes in research and advocacy around environmental health. Their reports and guides help consumers make informed decisions about the products they use and the food they eat.

Each of these organizations provides myriad resources tailored to various aspects of sustainable living. From DIY guides on home retrofits to large-scale campaigns for systemic change, these resources are treasure troves of actionable insights. Do take advantage of their newsletters, downloadable content, and social media updates.

Additionally, many organizations host webinars, online courses, and local events that not only educate but build a sense of community among like-minded individuals. Participating in these events can deepen your understanding of complex environmental issues while also extending your network of eco-conscious peers.

Don't forget the power of personal connection either. Networking with people who share your passion for the environment can be incredibly empowering. By joining local chapters or attending events sponsored by these organizations, you can meet people who are just as dedicated to sustainability. These interactions can spark collaborations, generate new ideas, and keep your motivation levels high.

For those wanting to take their involvement a step further, consider environmental advocacy training programs. Organizations like the Sierra Club and Greenpeace offer specialized training to equip you with the skills needed to lead your own campaigns, effectively communicate with lawmakers, and mobilize communities for environmental action.

Lastly, public libraries and community centers often have bulletin boards brimming with information on local eco-events, meetings, and volunteer opportunities. Spend a few minutes here; a simple flyer might lead you to an incredible opportunity for local involvement.

In wrapping up this section, remember that being part of a community—whether local or global—magnifies your impact. While individual actions are essential, collective effort transforms initiatives into movements, turning hope into tangible change. You're not alone on this journey; these organizations are there to support and guide you every step of the way.

Your hands, mind, and heart, combined with those of others, can create a wave of positive change. Reach out, get involved, and watch the ripple effect of your actions make the world a more sustainable place.

www.ingramcontent.com/pod-product-compliance
Lightning Source LLC
Chambersburg PA
CBHW020435290526
45785CB00002B/859